What Readers Are Saying About *Pragmatic Guide to Sass 3*

Sass is the abstraction that CSS needs. You would do well to learn it, and learn it well, by reading this book.

➤ **Chris Coyier**
Creator, CodePen

How better to learn about the features of Sass than from the guy who came up with it in the first place? Hampton, along with Michael, do a fantastic job of explaining the basics of Sass, then they go all the way up to the more advanced features. They even show some of the new, modern frameworks and techniques to help take Sass further. Definitely worth a read for beginners and advanced Sass developers alike.

➤ **Jina Bolton**
Lead designer, Salesforce Lightning Design System

Pragmatic Guide to Sass 3 is the quintessential book on Sass written by two of the only authors qualified to write such a definitive work. If you are new to Sass, this is the first book that you should read. If you are a Sass veteran, this book will become your go-to reference guide.

➤ **Micah Godbolt**
Author, *Frontend Architecture for Design Systems*

Sass is one of the most exciting web technologies to date, and whether you are brand-new to front-end development or a seasoned veteran of the web, you'll gain an in-depth look at the intricacies of how Sass works and all of its latest features in this book. *Pragmatic Guide to Sass 3* is a must-read for web developers and designers of all stripes.

➤ **Smith Schwartz**
UX engineer and Sasstronaut

Pragmatic Guide to Sass 3

Tame the Modern Style Sheet

Hampton Lintorn Catlin
Michael Lintorn Catlin

The Pragmatic Bookshelf

Raleigh, North Carolina

Our Pragmatic books, screencasts, and audio books can help you and your team create better software and have more fun. Visit us at *https://pragprog.com*.

The team that produced this book includes:

Brian P. Hogan (editor)
Potomac Indexing, LLC (index)
Nicole Abramowitz (copyedit)
Gilson Graphics (layout)
Janet Furlow (producer)

For sales, volume licensing, and support, please contact *support@pragprog.com*.

For international rights, please contact *rights@pragprog.com*.

Printed in the United States of America.
ISBN-13: 978-1-68050-176-6
Printed on acid-free paper.
Book version: P1.0—July 2016

Contents

Part I — Language Basics

Part II — Simple Use Cases

Part III — Advanced Mixins

Part IV — Values in Sass

Part V — Advanced Language Features

Part VI — Libraries and Frameworks

Acknowledgments

Writing this edition has been a joy, no doubt due to our editor, Brian Hogan, and managing editor, Susannah Pfalzer. The whole Pragmatic Programmers team makes it a wonderful experience to write a book.

We'd like to thank our tech reviewers: Nick Capito, Javier Collado, Peter Hampton, Nick McGinness, Nouran Mhmoud, Stephen Orr, Loren Sands-Ramshaw, Matthew Sullivan, Mitchell Volk, and Matthew White.

Hampton: Sass wouldn't exist today without Natalie Weizenbaum and Chris Eppstein. Their hard work and determination have made Sass the powerhouse developer tool that it is today.

Michael: I can't thank the Sass community enough. It's a pleasure to be part of such a supporting and welcoming group of people.

Welcome!

Welcome to the *Pragmatic Guide to Sass 3*. Sass (Syntactically Awesome Style Sheets) enables you to do amazing things with your style sheets and write more efficient, beautiful, and maintainable code.

"What's wrong with regular ol' CSS?" we hear you cry. The fact is that CSS, with all its power and elegance, is not designed for developer productivity. Instead, it's focused on helping the browser quickly display styles as simply as possible. There's nothing wrong with that, but it's not helpful for us as developers. That's where Sass comes in — to *extend* CSS, adding new features and syntax focused on making your life as a developer easier.

Sass isn't a replacement for CSS — it's a way to help us write *better* CSS files, which is essential for large projects. Sass helps us write clear, semantic style sheets. Sass updates our CSS development for the future. It's why our motto is "CSS with Superpowers."

Sass is by far the most popular of the CSS extension languages, according to almost every survey. It's used in almost every major web project and is the basis for most modern open source style frameworks.

Sass was originally conceived in 2006 as a component of the Haml templating language, and it was the first CSS extension language. It was initially envisaged by Hampton Lintorn Catlin, but it was primarily implemented by Natalie Weizenbaum, who has also been primarily responsible for the language's advanced features and serves as the primary language designer today. Chris Eppstein rounds out the language core team, being best known for Compass and Eyeglass, two popular Sass-related projects. We'll talk more about Eyeglass later. Sass has grown up a lot since that original concept! In fact, there are now multiple implementations of Sass, and it's available on most platforms.

In this book, we'll be using the word Sass as an overarching concept that describes the engine we use to convert our files into CSS. We can use two syntaxes to write Sass—SCSS and Original Sass. We'll describe these a bit later in this preface.

Who Is This Book For?

This book is for people who know the pain of working on the CSS of a mature website—who have faced a CSS file that four people wrote and that mutated into a huge, sprawling, incoherent mess. We've looked the beast in the eye and barely survived.

You're probably already familiar with CSS, HTML, and web development. We'll assume that you're familiar with margins, padding, the box model, @media queries, and myriad other CSS-related technologies.

If you're looking for a CSS ninja power-up, you've come to the right place.

Nomenclature and Syntax

Some of the terms associated with CSS can be confusing, so we've added a short introduction to how we name things in the book. Also, we've distinguished between the two different syntaxes for writing Sass.

A Brief CSS Recap

We thought it would be useful to go through a couple of technical terms we'll be using for different aspects of CSS markup. If you're already familiar with selectors, declaration blocks, and the like, you can probably skip this part.

Let's use a small bit of CSS as an example:

```
p {
  color: #336699;
  font-size: 2em;
}
```

Here we have p, which we call the *selector*. What follows (the bit inside the curly braces) is the *declaration block*. The two lines—one defining the color and one defining the font size—are known as *declarations*. Each declaration has a *property* and a *value*. The property in this case is the color or the font size. The value is the color itself—for example, *#336699*, blue—or the size of the font—for example, *2em*.

The use of *classes* and *IDs* allows us to define sets of declarations that will only be applied to specific sections of our HTML. Sass allows us to create much richer selectors, as we'll see in Part I, *Language Basics*, on page 3.

SCSS? Sass? Indented Sass?

You'll see the preceding terms used around the Internet, and it can be a little confusing what they're talking about. "Do you prefer Sass or SCSS?" is a common question you might get asked...and it is actually a nonsensical question! Here's why: Sass was originally an indented language. It has all the same concepts as CSS, but the syntax was more inspired by the Haml language than by CSS.

Later, the Sass team realized that the indented syntax was difficult for new users to grasp, so we created an alternate syntax for Sass. This alternate syntax is a strict subset of CSS, known as *SCSS (Sassy CSS)*. People often get confused and think that SCSS is an entirely different project or language from *Sass*. The truth is that both syntaxes are supported, and both make up the language of *Sass*. When we refer to the original syntax, we refer to it as *indented Sass* to make the distinction clear.

When someone is referring to Sass today, they're most likely referring to either the project itself or a file written in the SCSS syntax. There is usually no need to use the word SCSS unless you're being very specific about the syntax itself...it's all just Sass!

Typically, the extension for indented Sass is .sass, and the extension for SCSS is .scss—furthering the confusion about whether something is considered a Sass file or not. Both of those file extensions are considered Sass extensions, and they are how we tell the Sass compiler what syntax to expect.

We do plan on continuing to support the indented syntax into the future, and you can mix and match syntaxes across projects. In this book, we won't be using indented Sass at all. The indented syntax is far less common now. However, if you're interested in learning about indented Sass, a lot of good resources are available online for you to browse. All the code in this book will still work the same way, just with syntax variations.

Here's a quick summary of the main differences between the two syntaxes. Indented Sass has no parentheses or semicolons, whereas the SCSS syntax does. Here's a quick example comparing the two.

Indented syntax:

```
.modal
  color: #336699
  font-size: 2em
  a
    text-decoration: none
```

SCSS syntax:

```
.modal {
  color: #336699;
  font-size: 2em;
  a {
    text-decoration: none;
  }
}
```

The SCSS syntax, while a little more verbose, usually feels a lot more familiar to coders who are used to CSS syntax. That's why we're using it for our code examples in this book.

Overview

In Part I, *Language Basics*, on page 3, we'll take you through the first things you'll need to know about Sass, like how to install (Task 1, *Installing Sass*, on page 4). You'll also read about some of the core features of Sass, such as nesting (Task 2, *Scoping Selectors with Nesting*, on page 6), variables (Task 7, *Defining Variables*, on page 16), and mixins (Task 8, *Keeping Code Clean with Mixins*, on page 18).

In Part II, *Simple Use Cases*, on page 23, you'll learn about some real-world applications of Sass, such as better @media handling (Task 12, *Using Media Queries*, on page 30) and creating color themes (Task 10, *Creating Themes with Advanced Colors*, on page 26).

You'll dive deeper into mixins in Part III, *Advanced Mixins*, on page 37, looking at passing in arguments (Task 14, *Adding Mixin Arguments*, on page 38) and gating logic (Task 16, *Controlling Flow with @if*, on page 42).

In Part IV, *Values in Sass*, on page 51, things will get a little more technical. To grasp some of Sass's most advanced features, you'll learn about value types (Task 19, *Understanding Value Types in Sass*, on page 52). Then you can really get to grips with lists (Task 21, *Using Lists to Work with Multiple Properties*, on page 56) and maps (Task 24, *Using Maps for More Detailed Collections*, on page 62) in Sass.

In Part V, *Advanced Language Features*, on page 73, you'll learn about advanced features of Sass. In particular, you'll see how to use @extend (Task 31, *Using @extend as a Mixin Alternative*, on page 80), but you'll also see how to create functions (Task 28, *Creating Your Own Functions*, on page 74) and use the @at-root function (Task 34, *Escaping Indentation with @root*, on page 86).

Finally, in Part VI, *Libraries and Frameworks*, on page 91, you'll learn that sometimes it's more productive to look to libraries for help in creating a well-rounded website. You'll learn about some grid frameworks (Task 36, *Using Grid Systems for Layout*, on page 94) and Eyeglass (Task 37, *Introducing Eyeglass*, on page 96), a modular system to extend Sass's features.

How to Read This Book

The book is arranged into tasks. These are short snippets of information. You'll find a description of the task and on the next page will be the code you need to write to get results.

We've tried to arrange the book to go from basic to advanced tasks. However, you can definitely dip in and out of the book if you find a specific task you need to look at. Once you've grasped the basics (such as installing), you should be set to do most of the tasks in the book.

Getting Help

There are several ways you can find help for your Sass troubles; Sass has a warm and welcoming community, and we love helping people. For example, Stack Overflow is a great place to ask questions and find answers.[1] The Sass documentation has a wealth of information that covers most of what we look at in this guide and even goes over a few other things as well.[2]

In addition, if you ever need help with the sass command, just type sass --help, and Sass will let you know about all the available ways to run it.

A Few Final Comments

We're almost ready to start, but here are some little bits that you'll find useful to know before we dive into the book.

- We'll be using the following phrase to show when we've converted some Sass into CSS:

  This compiles to:

  Hopefully, you'll be familiar with the CSS output, so you can see how much simpler Sass is compared to CSS.

- If you've downloaded the ebook, you'll notice that all the code samples are preceded by a little shaded box. If you click the box, the code sample shown in the book will be downloaded to your computer, allowing you to play around with our examples.

- You can get more information from the book's official web page.[3] There you'll find resources such as the book forum, code downloads, and any errata.

OK—now that we've got all that out of the way, are you ready to get Sassy?

---

1. http://stackoverflow.com/questions/tagged/sass
2. http://sass-lang.com/docs/yardoc/file.SASS_REFERENCE.html
3. http://pragprog.com/book/pg_sass/pragmatic-guide-to-sass

Part I

Language Basics

Let's get started! This part will cover installing Sass and writing your first bits of Sass. Here's a quick rundown of what you'll be going through in the Basics section:

- You'll look at several ways to install Sass in Task 1, *Installing Sass*, on page 4.

- In Task 2, *Scoping Selectors with Nesting*, on page 6, you'll learn about one of the first—and most useful—features of Sass.

- In Task 3, *Commenting*, on page 8, you'll add comments that appear in the output, as well as comments that only appear in the source files.

- Then you'll learn about other features of scoping in Task 4, *Advanced Scoping*, on page 10.

- Next, you'll control the CSS produced by your compiler in Task 5, *CSS Output Styles*, on page 12.

- You'll put your code into separate files in Task 6, *Importing Files*, on page 14.

- Then you'll use some variables in Task 7, *Defining Variables*, on page 16.

- Finally, you'll get to know about mixins in Task 8, *Keeping Code Clean with Mixins*, on page 18.

1   Installing Sass

Sass can be installed in thousands of ways. Depending on your preferred language or operating system, you'll be able to find a suitable option to install it. There are so many ways to do this that we can't go over them all here. Search for your preferred language and Sass to get a good idea of what's out there. For example, there's a node-sass version if you like using Node. In this chapter, you'll learn about a couple of common methods. If you're already working on a project that involves Sass, feel free to skip this section.

If you're not comfortable with the command line, you have a couple of options. One is avoiding installation at all by using the great website SassMeister.[4] All you need to do is type your Sass on the input to the left, and the website automatically converts it into CSS for you!

Another great option is using Scout.[5] Scout is an application that works on Mac and Windows, and it helps compile Sass into CSS. It's as simple as pointing the app to our input scss file and indicating where we want the output css file to be placed. Easy!

If you're using Rails,[6] you don't need to do anything! Sass comes preinstalled with Rails projects, and it works on all platforms.

Installing (and using) Sass directly from the command line is slightly more complex. If you're familiar with the command line, though, it gives you the most flexibility. You can use the Ruby version of Sass and install the Sass gem—this works great on OSX as Ruby comes preinstalled.

If you prefer Node, you can install node-sass instead. Make sure that Node is installed on your machine,[7] then install the node-sass package.

To compile Sass from the command line, use the sass command (or node-sass, depending on how you installed Sass), as shown in the example. Pass in the file you want to compile followed by where the output should be.

---

4.   http://www.sassmeister.com/
5.   https://mhs.github.io/scout-app/
6.   https://rubygems.org/gems/rails
7.   https://nodejs.org/en/download/

➤ Use Ruby gems to install and compile Sass.

```
gem install sass
sass input.scss output.css
```

➤ Use Node to install and compile Sass.

```
npm install node-sass -g
node-sass --include-path scss input.scss output.css
```

Related Tasks:

- Task 37, *Introducing Eyeglass,* on page 96

2 Scoping Selectors with Nesting

One of the first features incorporated into Sass was the ability to nest selectors. If you've been working with CSS for a long time, you know the advantages of giving more specific selectors to your style sheets. Using .sidebar p em allows you greater specificity to the em element vs. a stand-alone em selector. It gives you more freedom with reusing names and making your HTML more semantic and readable. This is called *scoping*.

It's a good thing to scope, except it's repetitive. We have to repeat our classes or IDs. In the example on the next page, an apply-to-all class like .infobox is repeated—on every line. Typing this by hand is laborious and makes you want to streamline the process, doesn't it? When writing CSS, scoping can be tedious. It involves a lot of copying and pasting. What's more, keeping track of parent-child relationships is tough. We can do better than that! Technology should support good behaviors. Sass is here to help you with *nesting*.

You can put a style, such as a border color, *inside* a declaration block, and Sass will automatically do the repetitive part for you when you generate CSS. I bet your fingers are thanking you already for saving all that typing. Cool, huh?

A small note: the CSS that's compiled in the example on the next page looks a bit funny, doesn't it? Especially when you compare it to the original (repetitive) CSS example you wrote out. What happens is that the Sass engine keeps the indentation when it converts to CSS. All it does is insert the missing selectors.

➤ Look at this scoped CSS.

Check out all the repetition in this file. Holy cow!

basics/scoping.css

```
.infobox                    { width: 200px; }
.infobox .message           { border: 1px solid red; }
.infobox .message .title    { color: red; }
.infobox .user              { border: 2px solid black; }
.infobox .user .title       { color: black; }
```

➤ See it in Sass.

Instead of repeating it, nest it inside the parent selector.

basics/example_nesting.scss

```
.infobox {
  width: 200px;
  .message {
    border: 1px solid red;
    .title {
      color: red; } }
  .user {
    border: 2px solid black;
    .title {
      color: black; } } }
```

This compiles to:

```
.infobox {
  width: 200px;
}
.infobox .message {
  border: 1px solid red;
}
.infobox .message .title {
  color: red;
}
.infobox .user {
  border: 2px solid black;
}
.infobox .user .title {
  color: black;
}
```

Related Tasks:

- Task 4, *Advanced Scoping,* on page 10

3   Commenting

Well-commented code is essential for any project. From a team of just one all the way to a team of hundreds, comments help outline what code is supposed to do.

A comment is like an aside in your code—it can explain goals, indicate bug fixes, or just let someone know how you're using a particularly novel bit of code. And don't think that a solo project doesn't need comments! Some of the most valuable comments in our code are from our past selves.

Sass has two types of comment style. One is kept intact during compilation, so it appears in your CSS output. It's a multiline comment style, and you place all your comments between /* and */. This can be useful for versioning your CSS file or indicating the date it was compiled.

You can also keep your comments more private by preventing them from appearing in your CSS output. You can achieve this using the single-line comment style. At the start of every comment, use //.

➤ Comment using one of two styles.

In Sass, you can write:

basics/commenting.scss

```scss
/* Here's a comment that we're making
 * multiline and it's fine to show up
 * in our CSS output. */
button {
  color: #999;
}

// These are single line comments
// and we do not want them to appear
// in our CSS output.

button.sidebar {
  color: #DDD;
}
```

This compiles to:

```css
/* Here's a comment that we're making
 * multiline and it's fine to show up
 * in our CSS output. */
button {
  color: #999;
}

button.sidebar {
  color: #DDD;
}
```

4   Advanced Scoping

In Task 2, *Scoping Selectors with Nesting*, on page 6, we introduced selector nesting. Just throw a selector inside a declaration block and BAM! It automatically scopes the style as being the child of the parent. However, sometimes you need to be more explicit. The last example didn't specify that the children were *direct* children. In standard CSS, you can specify this directness as parent > child. If your CSS is rusty, that means finding a tag named <child>, which is exactly one level inside of a <parent> tag.

Using these kinds of CSS operators in Sass is as simple as you'd hope. As you can see in the example, a child selector can start with a > inside of the parent definition. Conversely, a parent can end with a >, affecting *all* of its children.

Using nesting is a great way to organize your styles. It means that all related styles are grouped together. By default, every child selector is the parent selector *plus* the child selector. In situations where you want to control how selectors are merged, you can use the & selector. Simply put, & means "the parent selector." Don't look scared. It's easy stuff once it clicks.

This can be useful when the <body> tag has a class that affects styles throughout the site. For instance, you may have an optional sidebar that affects the layout of content across the site. The <body> will have a class .has-sidebar when the sidebar is present. So when you're styling the content, you might want to add a rule that says, "If the body tag has this class, apply this rule," and it would be nice to have this code near all the related rules. So if you're inside of .infobox .item and then you write the child selector body.has-sidebar &, Sass will compile into body.has-sidebar .infobox .item.

The ampersand got replaced with .infobox .item, which was the parent's scope. If it's still a bit foggy, read over the examples. Then it should click. It really is simple!

➤ Define direct descendants.

basics/direct_descendants.scss

```scss
.infobox > {
  .message {
    > .title {
      color: red; } }
    .user {
    > .title {
      color: black; } } }
```

This compiles to:

```scss
.infobox > .message > .title {
  color: red;
}
.infobox > .user > .title {
  color: black;
}
```

➤ Reference ancestor selectors.

basics/ampersand_example.scss

```scss
.infobox {
  color: blue;
  .user & {
    color: gray; } }
.message {
  color: gray;
  &.new {
    color: red; } }
.infobox {
  body.has-sidebar & .message {
    content: "body.has-sidebar .infobox .message"; } }
```

This compiles to:

```scss
.infobox {
  color: blue;
}
.user .infobox {
  color: gray;
}
.message {
  color: gray;
}
.message.new {
  color: red;
}
body.has-sidebar .infobox .message {
  content: "body.has-sidebar .infobox .message"; }
```

5 CSS Output Styles

When you compile your Sass, a CSS file is generated. But what if you want that CSS file to be in a different format? If you compile your Sass on the command line, you have a few options to choose from. This means you can have your CSS output in a style that *you* prefer.

If you installed the Ruby version of Sass, in the command line, you can type this:

```
sass --style
```

If you installed the Node version of Sass, you can type this instead:

```
node-sass --output-style
```

Follow this with the name of the style you want. The four options you can choose from are called *nested, expanded, compact,* and *compressed.* For example, here's how you would use the Ruby version of Sass to output a compressed file:

```
sass --style compressed input.scss output.css
```

Nested is the default output style. It looks much like regular CSS, with curly braces and semicolons. This can be useful when you're developing a site and need to reference the output CSS regularly.

Expanded is, as its name suggests, an expanded form of the CSS output. All classes—including nested ones—expand rather than remaining nested in their parents. Both nested and expanded styles are probably the easiest to read, but they also have the largest file sizes.

Compact puts all the properties of a selector on one line, so it's easier to scan down a list of selectors.

Finally, compressed is possibly the most difficult to read. All spaces are removed, so the CSS sits on one line. This makes a compressed CSS file the smallest, which is great for mobile devices, for example.

➤ Check out the Sass we'll be compiling in each case.

basics/outputs.scss

```
.infobox {
  .message {
    border: 1px solid red;
    background: #336699;
    .title {
      color: red; } } }
```

➤ Nested (the default setting) looks like this:

```
.infobox .message {
  border: 1px solid red;
  background: #336699; }
  .infobox .message .title {
    color: red; }
```

➤ Expanded looks like this:

```
.infobox .message {
  border: 1px solid red;
  background: #336699;
}
.infobox .message .title {
  color: red;
}
```

➤ Compact looks like this:

```
.infobox .message { border: 1px solid red;
                              background: #336699; }
.infobox .message .title { color: red; }
```

(The first declaration should be on one line.)

➤ Compressed looks like this:

```
.infobox .message{border:1px solid red;background:#336699} ➤
    .infobox .message .title{color:red}
```

(The compressed output didn't fit on one line in the book, so we had to create another one. In the real thing, though, it is all on one line.)

6   Importing Files

When you're developing, it's often useful to have many smaller style sheets rather than one huge one. Who wants to read through a thousand-line style sheet? However, loading many small CSS files can be a pain for web performance. If you have five style sheets on a particular page, it can make the page-loading times much slower because each style sheet needs a separate request to load.

Importing is a process by which a lot of files are turned into a few files. Sass has a neat little trick whereby the smaller style sheets are imported into the larger one as it is compiled into CSS. All you need to type is @import, followed by the name of the Sass file you want to import. You can mix Original Sass and SCSS at will with imports—it's all the same. Just say @import "sub_page"; and you're done!

By default, the Sass compiler generates CSS files from all your .sass files—even the "small" ones. If you don't want a Sass file to generate a corresponding CSS file, just start the filename with an underscore (if you're familiar with Rails, this is a bit like doing a Rails partial). For example, you can name the file _sub_page.scss. In the import line, you can leave off the underscore. If you don't mind that a separate style sheet is created for the child page, you can name it sub_page.scss.

It's as simple as that. Any *variables* or *mixins* (you'll learn about those later) you used in the imported style sheet can be used in the parent file too. Note that you must import all the definitions of variables *before* you use them in your style sheet.

➤ Create separate files.

basics/_buttons.scss

```
button {
  background: #336699;
}
```

basics/header.scss

```
header {
  height: 100px;
}
```

➤ Import into the main file.

basics/importing.scss

```
@import "buttons";
@import "header";

a {
  color: green;
}
```

(You don't need to include the underscore or extension with _buttons.scss.)

This compiles to:

```
button {
  background: #336699; }
header {
  height: 100px; }
a {
  color: green; }
```

Remember the rule about the underscores—when we compile into CSS, the two imported files will not be treated the same. The header.scss file will create its own separate CSS file because it doesn't start with an underscore.

7   Defining Variables

Have you ever been in a situation where you are copying the value of a color over and over again? That specific blue appears in so many places. Then, a couple of weeks later, you need to change the color. Or—even worse—you have a whole lot of colors to change. Find-and-replace time!

Sass introduces variables to help us manage problems like this. All variables in Sass are prefixed with a $ sign. Assigning a variable looks a lot like typing in a CSS property. For instance, you can set the $primary_color variable by adding the super-simple line: $primary_color: #369;. That's it!

To use the variable, just use the variable name where you'd usually use the property value. If you have to change the colors of the whole document, you only need to change the hex value of the variable; it will be sorted for you when the CSS compiles.

You can use variables to represent colors, sizes, percents, and several other things that are less commonly used. Anything that you can put to the right of a CSS property is easily understood by Sass. Another great usage for variables is assigning a series of fonts to them.

Another neat thing about variables is they can be *global* or *scoped*. The variables we've looked at so far have been global. Global variables are defined on their own line and apply to the whole style sheet. Scoped variables, on the other hand, appear within a selector and only apply to that selector and its children.

You can set default variables with the !default tag after assignment. When a variable is used, the default is used if there are no other assignments to that variable.

It's pretty standard in a Sass document to declare the variables at the top of a file and use them throughout. Or, if you have a large project, you might want to create a file (or multiple files!) that defines all of the variables. Then, just import it as we learned in the previous task.

➤ Define, then use variables.

basics/variables.scss

```
$header-background: #EEE;
$link-color: #369;
$menu-width: 300px;

header {
  // Set the background to be #EEE
  background: $header-background;
  .menu {
    width: $menu-width;
    background: white;
    a {
      color: $link-color; } } }
```

This compiles to:

```
header {
  background: #EEE;
}
header .menu {
  width: 300px;
  background: white;
}
header .menu a {
  color: #369;
}
```

Related Tasks:

- Task 9, *Calculating a Simple Layout*, on page 24

8   Keeping Code Clean with Mixins

Mixins are some of the more powerful elements of Sass. A mixin is a fragment of Sass that can easily be applied to another selector. Let's say you require a distinct style for alerts: red text with small caps. You need to apply this style to many alerts in your document. You don't want to have to repeat color: #AE2F2F; over and over again. This is the perfect situation for a mixin!

To define a mixin, all you need to type is @mixin, followed by the name of the mixin and then its styling.

Once you've defined it, you can easily use a mixin wherever you please—it's a super-portable set of attributes. A mixin can include far more data than a simple variable. When you want to use the mixin, just type @include.

Mixins also help you keep your code semantic. You can define a mixin as alert-text, then apply it to a class with a more specific name, such as input-error.

It's useful to have mixins in a separate style sheet, keeping your main style sheet cleaner. If this is the case, you need to use the bundling technique—put @import at the top of your main Sass file, linking in the mixins file.

Depending on whether you're using indented Sass or SCSS, the use of mixins is slightly different. We've been through the SCSS way, where we describe a mixin with @mixin and use it with @include. With indented Sass, you use = before the mixin description and use + instead of the @include command.

➤ Define a mixin.

basics/define_mixin.scss

```
@mixin alert-text {
  color: #AE2F2F;
  font-size: 14px;
  font-variant: small-caps;
}
```

➤ Use a mixin.

basics/use_mixin.scss

```
@import "define_mixin";
.input-error {
  @include alert-text;
  margin-bottom: 10px;
}
```

This compiles to:

```
.input-error {
  color: #AE2F2F;
  font-size: 14px;
  font-variant: small-caps;
  margin-bottom: 10px;
}
```

Related Tasks:

- Task 14, *Adding Mixin Arguments*, on page 38
- Task 15, *Using More Mixin Argument Tricks*, on page 40
- Task 17, *Manipulating @content*, on page 44
- Task 16, *Controlling Flow with @if*, on page 42

Part II

Simple Use Cases

Taking what you've learned in *Language Basics*, you're going to expand on it by applying those Sass techniques to some common situations.

- Firstly, in Task 9, *Calculating a Simple Layout*, on page 24, you'll use some Sass math for a layout.

- Then, in Task 10, *Creating Themes with Advanced Colors*, on page 26, you'll learn about some of Sass's power with colors.

- You'll use Sass to create a handy reset file in Task 11, *Resetting CSS*, on page 28.

- Then, you'll organize @media queries with Sass in Task 12, *Using Media Queries*, on page 30.

- Lastly, you'll explore ways to organize your style sheets in Task 13, *Organizing Your Style Sheets*, on page 32.

9   Calculating a Simple Layout

Sass allows you to do calculations on the fly and in your document: you can easily type width: 12px * 0.5; in your code!

…

OK, OK—we admit that's not terribly useful. But it is once you throw variables into the mix. Once you've defined a variable, Sass allows you to perform basic operations on that variable using standard operators for adding, subtracting, multiplying, and dividing (+, -, *, and /). The operators will be familiar to anyone who has done any amount of programming before.

You could say something like width: $page_width * 0.1 as a way to avoid hard-coding pixel values. When the CSS is compiled, this will be pre-calculated and will print out an exact width in pixels.

You can now do the previously laborious tasks such as calculating and maintaining proportions throughout a layout.

For example, you can define the width of the content area of the page as 500px. Then you can base the width of the sidebar as a proportion of the total width—say, 0.2. If you want to change the size of the content area, the sidebar can automatically resize itself to fit. All it takes is variables plus some operator know-how.

A quick note about units here. If you define $page_width as *10em* and you multiply it by two, the resulting value will keep the em unit. The same goes if it were px. If you mix units, Sass will try to make them work, but if they are incompatible, Sass will display an error. For instance, you can't multiply a px value by a em value. It just doesn't make sense.

➤ Add, subtract, multiply, or divide using the standard operators.

simpleusecases/layout_math.scss

```
$width:         10px;
$double_width:  $width * 2;
$half_width:    $width / 2;
$width_plus_2:  $width + 2;
$width_minus_2: $width - 2;
```

➤ Use calculations inline.

simpleusecases/layout_calculations.scss

```
$width: 500px;
$sidebar_percent: 0.2;

.page {
  width: $width;
  .sidebar {
    width: $width * $sidebar_percent; }
  .content {
    width: $width * (1 - $sidebar_percent); } }
```

This compiles to:

```
.page {
  width: 500px;
}
.page .sidebar {
  width: 100px;
}
.page .content {
  width: 400px;
}
```

Related Tasks:

• Task 7, *Defining Variables,* on page 16

10   Creating Themes with Advanced Colors

Making and altering a color palette for a site can be a pain. Going into hex charts to find a slightly lighter color can feel like stabbing around in the dark.

Thankfully, Sass comes with a wealth of functions to make manipulating color more precise. There's lighten and darken, and saturate and desaturate; and there's a whole bunch more in Appendix 1, *SassScript Function Reference*, on page 103.

There are many books on color theory that can explain relationships, but we'll go over some handy functions here. For example, *complement($color)* is a function that returns the complementary color for the input you specify.

The *desaturate($color, $amount)* function allows you to create more neutral tones from a primary color, whereas *saturate($color, $amount)* creates a more vivid, bold color. It can be useful to use more neutral colors for most of a site, with pops of more saturated color to draw attention to certain areas.

The *mix($color1, $color2, [$weight])* function takes two arguments: the colors you want to mix. Instead of picking colors at random for a more diverse color palette, mix your two primary colors then play around with saturation and lightness. This makes a theme more coherent.

Another handy way to use color functions is to create your black and white shades for a site. Using #FFF and #000 is not a best practice—it's bad for accessibility, and using absolutes is jarring to the eye. Instead, use *grayscale($color)* on a dark neutral to make a black, and use *lighten($color, $amount)* on an already light neutral to create a white.

For some great Sass functions that include a lot of the ideas and processes described here, check out Natalya Shelburne's guide to color theory. [8]

---

8.   http://tallys.github.io/color-theory/

➤ Desaturate colors to create neutrals.

```
$primary-color: #336699;
.page {
  color: desaturate($primary-color, 30%); }
```

This compiles to:

```
.page {
  color: #52667A; }
```

➤ Lighten/darken colors.

```
.page {
  color: lighten(#336699, 20%); }
```

This compiles to:

```
.page {
  color: #6699cc; }
```

➤ Create blacks and whites with grayscale.

```
grayscale(#336699);
```

Using this method is the same as typing this:

```
desaturate(#336699, 100%);
```

➤ Mix colors.

This function allows you to mix colors:

```
.page {
  color: mix(#336699, #993266); }
```

Mixing blue and red gives a beautiful purple:

```
color: #664C80;
```

➤ Change the hue.

We use the adjust-hue function, followed by the number of degrees we want to rotate the hue.

```
$primary-color: #336699;
.page {
  color: adjust-hue($primary-color, 180); }
.page {
  color: adjust-hue(desaturate($primary-color, 10%), 90); }
```

11 Resetting CSS

A common technique to reset a style sheet is to override all of the default styles that browsers provide before you begin styling a site. This way, you won't accidentally assume, for instance, that all <h1> tags are the same font and font size between browsers. The default <h1> is different in Internet Explorer, Firefox, Safari... it's so annoying! To get around this, designers often employ a "reset CSS" file.

On the right, we've provided a Sass version of the most famous reset CSS file by Eric Meyer. It's shorter than the original CSS version.

You probably don't want to add all that boilerplate to the top of your master style sheet, so it's often more useful to employ the importing technique. Put the reset file into a separate style sheet named something like _reset.scss. Then at the start of the style sheet, put @import "reset"; and the reset is incorporated into the CSS file when it's compiled.

➤ Reset CSS.

```scss
/*
   Sass Reset - Converted by Hampton Lintorn Catlin
   A modification of the original found at...
   http://meyerweb.com/eric/tools/css/reset/
*/
html, body, div, span, applet, object, iframe, h1, h2, h3, h4,
h5, h6, p, blockquote, pre, a, abbr, acronym, address, big,
cite, code, del, dfn, em, img, ins, kbd, q, s, samp, small,
strike, strong, sub, sup, tt, var, b, u, i, center, dl, dt, dd,
ol, ul, li, fieldset, form, label, data, legend, table, colgroup,
caption, col, tbody, tfoot, thead, tr, th, td, article, aside,
param, canvas, details, embed, figure, figcaption, footer,
header, hgroup, main, menu, nav, output, ruby, section, summary,
time, mark, audio, video, source, track, map, area {
  margin: 0;
  padding: 0;
  border: 0;
  font-size: 100%;
  font: inherit;
  vertical-align: baseline; }
/* HTML5 display-role reset for older browsers */
article, aside, details, figcaption, figure, footer,
header, hgroup, menu, nav, section {
  display: block; }
body {
  line-height: 1; }
ol, ul {
  list-style: none; }
blockquote, q {
  quotes: none; }
blockquote {
  &:before, &:after {
    content: '';
    content: none; } }
q {
  &:before, &:after {
    content: '';
    content: none; } }
table {
  border-collapse: collapse;
  border-spacing: 0; }
```

Related Tasks:

- Task 6, *Importing Files,* on page 14

12 Using Media Queries

Media queries are essential tools in CSS for developing responsive web designs. They allow us to conditionally apply styles to a site based on the width of the browser—without relying on complex JavaScript.

Typically, when designing a responsive website, it's important to specify *size classes*. Size classes are a range of acceptable browser widths matched against styles for a site. For instance, you might say that less than 400px is considered the mobile-size class, while greater than 1200px is the large desktop-size class.

Sass makes it easier to define these style classes by allowing you to use variables with @media declarations. You can define, in one place, all your size classes and then use those variables throughout your style sheets. You can see this in the accompanying example.

Nesting—another great feature of Sass—works just great with media queries. In CSS 3, media queries are defined at the root of the document. This constraint means that the styles for size classes have to be defined far away from each other. With nesting, you can group them together in the same area. This makes your code far easier to read!

➤ Create a file for size classes.

simpleusecases/_size_classes.scss

```
$small-screen: 500px;
$medium-screen: 800px;
$large-screen: 1200px;
```

➤ Use nested @media with variables.

simpleusecases/atmedia.scss

```
@import "size_classes";

.information {
  color: #336699;
  line-height: 1em;
  @media (min-width: $medium-screen) {
    line-height: 1.5em; }
  @media (min-width: $large-screen) {
    line-height: 2em; } }
```

This compiles to:

```
.information {
  color: #336699;
  line-height: 1em;
}
@media (min-width: 800px) {
  .information {
    line-height: 1.5em;
  }
}
@media (min-width: 1200px) {
  .information {
    line-height: 2em;
  }
}
```

Related Tasks:

- Task 7, *Defining Variables*, on page 16
- Task 17, *Manipulating @content*, on page 44

13   Organizing Your Style Sheets

Back in *Importing Files*, you learned about how to split up one giant Sass style sheet into multiple smaller style sheets. Especially on larger projects, though, figuring out exactly *how* to split up your style sheets can be a problem. Here, you'll learn about some recommended ways to organize Sass.

Firstly, you should always have a base or main Sass file that contains all your imports. This gives you a nice central location where you can see all the other files you're importing. No Sass other than @import should be present in this file.

The structure of your Sass files should be centered around three core folders: globals, components, and pages. The globals folder should contain all the Sass files with global items—things such as your collections of colors, variables, and mixins. The variables file contains all variables that don't neatly fit into another category. If you're focusing on a re-sponsive site, then a media queries file would also be found in globals. The _reset.scss from *Resetting CSS* should also be found here.

The components folder should contain all Sass files relating to stand-alone components of a site. For example, the header and footer should have partial files in this folder. Finally, the pages folder should con-tain—you guessed it!—all page-specific styles.

Notice that in the example of a main.scss file, you import all the globals Sass files separately; but you import the components and pages all at once, using the neat * trick. You should import all the globals separately as they can be dependent on one another. You may use some colors or variables in the mixins file, for example, so their files must be im-ported before the _mixins.scss partial.

➤ Use the following folder structure to organize style sheets.

```
stylesheets/
  main.scss
  globals/
    _colors.scss
    _mixins.scss
    _variables.scss
  components/
    _header.scss
    _footer.scss
  pages/
    _register.scss
    _profile.scss
```

➤ Import all style sheets into one main file.

simpleusecases/main.scss

```
@import "globals/variables";
@import "globals/colors";
@import "globals/mixins";

@import "components/*";

@import "pages/*";
```

Related Tasks:

- Task 6, *Importing Files,* on page 14
- Task 11, *Resetting CSS,* on page 28

Part III

Advanced Mixins

You learned how to create a mixin in *Keeping Code Clean with Mixins*. However, mixins are far more powerful than what was described there. In this part, you'll dive deeper into all the features of mixins.

- You'll pass arguments into mixins in Task 14, *Adding Mixin Arguments*, on page 38.

- Then, you'll use a couple more argument tricks in Task 15, *Using More Mixin Argument Tricks*, on page 40.

- In Task 16, *Controlling Flow with @if*, on page 42, you'll control flow through a mixin.

- Then, you'll pass content into a mixin in Task 17, *Manipulating @content*, on page 44.

- Finally, you'll discover a common use case for mixins in Task 18, *Using Mixins for Cross-Browser Compatibility*, on page 46.

14   Adding Mixin Arguments

When you created mixins in *Keeping Code Clean with Mixins,* you placed all the necessary styles in the mixin itself. However, the true power of mixins comes with using arguments.

Say you have a general notice style that you'd like to use in a mixin. However, sometimes the notice is green, and sometimes it's red. Making two mixins seems a little unnecessary. You can use an argument instead! Instead of putting a predefined background in the mixin block, put $background (or whatever you wish to call it) in. Then, when naming the mixin, include the $background part in parentheses after the name.

In the example (which uses a much simpler mixin, but you get the idea), see that you can manipulate the arguments you pass in. The background being used is darkened in order to get a border color.

When using the mixin, just pass in the arguments in the order you defined them. You can also specify which argument is which by placing the name in front of the argument—these are called *keyword arguments.* You can see that in the second mixin use in the example. Although this looks a little more wordy, it helps for a couple of reasons. It means that you don't have to remember the exact order of arguments. It also makes your code easier to read. If you have two color-based arguments, for example, using the keyword can help you remember which argument you're referencing.

➤ Create a mixin with arguments.

advancedmixins/create_mixin.scss

```
@mixin notice-box($background, $width) {
  background: $background;
  border: 1px solid darken($background, 20%);
  width: $width;
}
```

➤ Use a mixin that takes arguments.

advancedmixins/use_mixin.scss

```
@import "create_mixin";
.warning {
  @include notice-box(red, 100%);
}
.welcome {
  @include notice-box($width: 300px, $background: green);
}
```

This compiles to:

```
.warning {
  background: red;
  border: 1px solid #990000;
  width: 100%; }

.welcome {
  background: green;
  border: 1px solid #001a00;
  width: 300px; }
```

Related Tasks:

- Task 8, *Keeping Code Clean with Mixins*, on page 18
- Task 15, *Using More Mixin Argument Tricks*, on page 40

15 Using More Mixin Argument Tricks

In some situations, you might want to set a default argument for a mixin. For example, in most cases, you want to have a default background. However, in some cases, you want to be able to set it yourself. In this situation, you can put a default value in the mixin, then you can change it if necessary.

You can set the default value to be null if necessary. In this case, when the mixin is compiled, it will leave out the value entirely—unless you specify one when including the mixin.

In the example, there is a default background and width for the mixin. In the header menu, it's fine that the background uses the default color. However, you might want to overwrite the default width with a new value. You can just pass that in when you're including the mixin! Simple.

Sometimes you want to pass in a variable number of arguments into a mixin. Some examples of where this would be useful are for shadows or gradients. box-shadow can take any number of shadows, and linear-gradient can merge together many colors.

To let a mixin know that there might be multiple arguments, just add three periods after the argument name when defining the mixin. In the example, that variable argument is being used in a linear-gradient function.

Then, the mixin is used twice—once with three colors and once with seven. The mixin handles the variable number of arguments easily!

➤ Create and use default arguments.

advancedmixins/default_mixin.scss

```
@mixin dropdown($background: #333, $width: 200px, $opacity: null) {
  background: $background;
  opacity: $opacity;
  padding: 10px 20px;
  width: $width;
}

.header-menu {
  @include dropdown($width: 300px);
}
```

This compiles to:

```
.header-menu {
  background: #333;
  padding: 10px 20px;
  width: 300px; }
```

➤ Use variable arguments.

advancedmixins/variable_arguments.scss

```
@mixin rainbow($colors...) {
  background: linear-gradient($colors)
}

.warm-rainbow {
  @include rainbow(red, orange, yellow);
}

.full-rainbow {
  @include rainbow(red, orange, yellow, green, blue, purple);
}
```

This compiles to:

```
.warm-rainbow {
  background: linear-gradient(red, orange, yellow); }

.full-rainbow {
  background: linear-gradient(red, orange, yellow, green, blue, purple); }
```

Related Tasks:

- Task 8, *Keeping Code Clean with Mixins,* on page 18
- Task 14, *Adding Mixin Arguments,* on page 38

16   Controlling Flow with @if

You can make your mixins even more powerful by making certain things happen only under specific circumstances. You do this using @if. This gating mechanism, also known as a *conditional statement*, is a common feature of programming languages, so you might be familiar with it.

To start your statement, you write the @if keyword. After that, you put a *statement* that will evaluate to true or false. For example, 20 > 10 would evaluate to true. And, "hello" == "world" would evaluate to false. Other common comparators are available, such as == (equal to), != (not equal to), > (greater than), and < (less than).

If the statement is true, whatever is inside the following declaration block will be executed. If the statement is false, then it will look for an @else as the next block to continue trying until it successfully matches. If it runs out of @else blocks, then it won't do anything at all.

In the example, there's a single mixin that produces two types of buttons. If you don't specify a shadow, the first block will run, creating a button with a border. However, if you *do* add a shadow when using the mixin, the @else statement will run, creating a button with a shadow instead of a border.

➤ Use @if to make more flexible mixins.

advancedmixins/atif_mixin.scss

```scss
@mixin button($background, $shadow: null) {
  background: $background;
  @if $shadow == null {
    border: 2px solid darken($background, 20%);
  } @else {
    box-shadow: $shadow;
  }
}
.flat-button {
  @include button(green);
}

.floating-button {
  @include button(red, 1px 0px 0px #999)
}
```

This compiles to:

```scss
.flat-button {
  background: green;
  border: 2px solid #001a00; }

.floating-button {
  background: red;
  box-shadow: 1px 0px 0px #999; }
```

Related Tasks:

• Task 8, *Keeping Code Clean with Mixins*, on page 18

17 Manipulating @content

Mixins can have full declaration blocks passed into them when they are included. When declaring the mixin, you can include the content that's passed in by using the *@content* directive.

This is useful for some complex mixins and libraries. It isn't used that often, but you can build some clever and useful mixins with it.

In the example, you want to style the page slightly differently if the summer sales attribute is on the body. You don't want to have to type out that long, ungainly selector every time you want to make a small adjustment to the styles. This is a perfect situation for passing in a content block! You can see in the mixin declaration that there's also an & to indicate the body rule should be at the top of the content block that's passed in.

Another way you could use @content is to simplify media queries. Sometimes it's difficult to remember if you should use max-width or min-width in your media query. To help, write a mixin called larger-than, which takes the size you need.

➤ Use @content to skip writing a long selector.

advancedmixins/atcontent.scss

```scss
@mixin sale-styles {
  body[data-selector="summer-sale"] & {
    @content;
  }
}
.sign-in {
  display: block;
  @include sale-styles {
    float: left;
  }
}
```

This compiles to:

```scss
.sign-in {
  display: block;
}
body[data-selector="summer-sale"] .sign-in {
  float: left;
}
```

➤ Create a simpler media mixin.

advancedmixins/atcontent_media.scss

```scss
@mixin larger-than($size) {
  @media (min-width: $size) {
    @content;
  }
}
.modal {
  @include larger-than(900px) {
    width: 500px; } }
```

Related Tasks:

• Task 8, *Keeping Code Clean with Mixins,* on page 18

18   Using Mixins for Cross-Browser Compatibility

We all love to use new and cutting-edge features in our style sheets. It's what keeps our websites looking slick! However, this often causes a headache, especially in CSS, due to *cross-browser compatibility*.

The main browsers (such as Internet Explorer, Firefox, and WebKit) implement some CSS rules differently. This means that you have to use those weird-looking CSS prefixes to make your styles work in all those places.

Using a Sass mixin is a perfect way to not have to write out those prefixes all the time. In the first example, there's an appearance mixin. It takes the value you need, and then you use that value in all the prefixed rules you need. Using the mixin is simple—just pass in the value you want to use!

In the second example, there's a slightly more complex situation: you need to prefix a pseudo-selector. Using the tricks you learned in *Manipulating @content*, you can pass in the declarations you want. Here, you're specifying how the placeholders for your input should look.

➤ Create a mixin for cross-browser prefixes.

advancedmixins/cross_browser.scss

```scss
@mixin appearance($value) {
  -webkit-appearance: $value;
  -moz-appearance: $value;
  appearance: $value;
}
header input {
  @include appearance(searchfield); }
```

This compiles to:

```css
header input {
  -webkit-appearance: searchfield;
  -moz-appearance: searchfield;
  appearance: searchfield; }
```

➤ Use @content for pseudo-selectors.

advancedmixins/cross_browser_content.scss

```scss
@mixin placeholder-styles() {
  &::-webkit-input-placeholder {
    @content;
  }
  &::-moz-placeholder {
    @content;
  }
  &:-ms-input-placeholder {
    @content;
  }
}
input {
  @include placeholder-styles {
    font-style: italic; } }
```

This compiles to:

```css
input::-webkit-input-placeholder {
  font-style: italic;
}
input::-moz-placeholder {
  font-style: italic;
}
input:-ms-input-placeholder {
  font-style: italic;
}
```

Related Tasks:

• Task 17, *Manipulating @content*, on page 44

Part IV

Values in Sass

Next up, you're going to learn about two of the most powerful data structures in Sass: lists and maps. They're important for many reasons, so let's get started!

- Firstly, you'll discover the concept of types in Task 19, *Understanding Value Types in Sass*, on page 52.

- In Task 20, *Interpolating*, on page 54, you'll create dynamic Sass.

- You'll take a closer look at lists in Task 21, *Using Lists to Work with Multiple Properties*, on page 56.

- You'll look at two ways to use lists in Task 22, *Looping Through Lists*, on page 58, and Task 23, *Manipulating Lists*, on page 60.

- In Task 24, *Using Maps for More Detailed Collections*, on page 62, you'll dive into another value type: maps.

- You'll use maps in Task 25, *Looping Through Maps*, on page 64, and Task 26, *Manipulating Maps*, on page 66.

- In Task 27, *Using Maps for Namespace Configuration*, on page 68, you'll see how to use maps to configure style sheets.

19   Understanding Value Types in Sass

Everything we write in Sass, from classes to pixel widths, can be considered a value. However, values can be of different *types*. This makes some aspects of them incompatible, and learning about their differences is essential for writing more complex Sass. In some cases, it's possible to convert from one value type to another with some special Sass functions. In this task, you'll learn about the types of values found in Sass, plus some conversion functions.

Numbers are pretty self-explanatory. Any time you write a digit in Sass, that's of the number type—even if it has a unit associated with it. So 12, 59.7%, and 200px are all numbers.

Colors are also straightforward. They can be hex values (for example, #336699) or RGB values (for example, rgb(120, 200, 89)).

Booleans are values that are true or false.

There's also a type called *null*, which you can use if something isn't present in your style sheet. You can see it being used in Task 16, *Controlling Flow with @if*, on page 42.

Strings can be considered to be everything else in Sass: class names, font names, and so on. We can convert to strings by using the *inspect($value)* function.

The final two value types, *lists* and *maps*, will be introduced in the next few tasks.

If you ever need to know what type a value is, use the handy function *type-of($value)*. It will return the type of your value! This can be useful in creating robust mixins. Say you have a border mixin that takes a color and a width, but everyone keeps on confusing the two arguments! You can test the arguments within the mixin to get their type, then use that type to determine if the argument should be used as a border-color or a border-width.

➤ Use inspect to convert to a string.

values/inspect.scss

```
inspect(200) /* Will return a string of "200" */
inspect(false) /* Will return a string of "false" */
```

➤ Use type-of for resilient mixins.

values/type_of.scss

```
@mixin border($argument1, $argument2) {
  @if type-of($argument1) == "color" {
    border-color: $argument1;
    border-width: $argument2;
  } @else {
    border-color: $argument2;
    border-width: $argument1;
  }
}
.alert {
  @include border(#369, 1px);
}
.button {
  @include border(4px, #F84)
}
```

Related Tasks:

- Task 21, *Using Lists to Work with Multiple Properties*, on page 56
- Task 24, *Using Maps for More Detailed Collections*, on page 62

20 Interpolating

Included in Sass are some programmer-style functions, which we'll look over in the next couple of tasks. These are called *SassScripts*.

Let's learn about a general SassScript that allows you to dynamically generate style sheets. It's called *interpolation*. Oh, fancy sounding word—how we love you! It makes us sound smart just by saying it. You try it: *interpolation*. Feels good, doesn't it?

Interpolation basically means "put this there." Imagine you want to write a mixin that has a dynamic property or selector. And you don't want a dynamic property value—that's easy stuff that you've already done. You want the very *name* of a property or selector to be dynamically generated. Well, you're in luck, because that's exactly what interpolation can do.

Just wrap the name of a variable in #{}, and you're done. For example, you could have #{$myvar}. The variable will be printed out wherever you put that. So, you could say .button-#{$type}. And, if $type is set to alert, it would generate the selector .button-alert. Wha-bam! Victory!

You can pretty much use interpolation anywhere you want in your Sass files. Go crazy! In the example, it's used in a mixin to generate some button classes. You can also use it in a filename.

➤ Interpolate to create a dynamic selector.

values/interpolation.scss

```scss
@mixin button($type, $color, $icon) {
  // Create a class with the button type
  .button-#{$type} {
    color: $color;
    width: 100px;
    .icon {
      background: url("images/#{$icon}.png");
    }
  }
}

@include button("alert",    "red",   "exclamation");
@include button("register", "green", "arrow");
```

This compiles to:

```css
.button-alert {
  color: "red";
  width: 100px;
}
.button-alert .icon {
  background: url("images/exclamation.png");
}

.button-register {
  color: "green";
  width: 100px;
}
.button-register .icon {
  background: url("images/arrow.png");
}
```

Related Tasks:

- Task 8, *Keeping Code Clean with Mixins*, on page 18
- Task 14, *Adding Mixin Arguments*, on page 38

21   Using Lists to Work with Multiple Properties

Lists are used in many places in Sass. In fact, Sass treats most values and properties as lists by default. For example, in the declaration padding: 10px 20px 5px 5px;, Sass assumes that the pixel values are a list of four items. Lists are just a series of items that can be separated by a comma or a space. Lists can even consist of just one item. Some great use cases for lists are keeping multiple font selections together, or creating a collection of colors that you need for a style guide.

You can select items in a list by using the *nth($list, $n)* function. It takes two arguments: the list of items, followed by the *index* of the item in the list. In Sass, index counting starts at 1.

The example uses some browser incompatibility to show how the nth function can be used. For border-radius, you can pass in two values—for example, border-radius: 20px 5px;. Those values will be treated as top-left/bottom-right (20px), and top-right/bottom-left (5px) radii. Yet, -webkit-border-radius treats two values differently: it assumes you want *all* the corners to be elliptical with a height of the first value (20px) and a width of the second (5px). To get the desired outcome with the We-bKit version, you need to explicitly state all four pixel values.

You can write a mixin to solve this. The mixin converts a "regular" border-radius with two values into a -webkit-border-radius by using the nth function to select particular values from the list you pass in.

You can also create lists of lists—for example, the first item in a list can itself be a list. In order not to confuse Sass (and to keep your code readable), you should wrap sublists in parentheses.

➤ Check out this example of a list.

```
$my-list: "20px, 5px, 100px, 40px";
```

➤ Use the nth() to expand a list.

values/lists.scss

```
@mixin border-radius($list) {
  border-radius: $list;
  -webkit-border-radius: nth($list, 1) nth($list, 2)
                         nth($list, 1) nth($list, 2);
}
.selector {
  @include border-radius(20px 5px)
}
```

This compiles to:

```
.selector {
  border-radius: 20px 5px;
  -webkit-border-radius: 20px 5px 20px 5px;
}
```

➤ Use parentheses to designate nested lists.

```
$spacing: ("20px, 5px"), ("10px, 15px"), ("30px, 40px");
```

Related Tasks:

- Task 22, *Looping Through Lists,* on page 58
- Task 23, *Manipulating Lists,* on page 60

22   Looping Through Lists

There are a few more Sass functions that allow us to interact with lists. The next one you'll learn about is @each.

@each allows you to loop through every item in a list. At that point, you can choose to do something with that item: for example, use interpolation to create a series of classes.

In the example, you can see a new way of setting up a list: assigning it to a variable. This is totally valid Sass and can definitely keep your mixins and functions clean.

You can loop through a list of colors in order to create a series of classes with appropriate colors assigned to them. Another handy way to use @each is to use a list of filenames to create a series of icon classes with their corresponding paths.

➤ Loop through a list using @each.

values/looping_lists.scss

```scss
$colors: "red", "green", "blue";

@each $color in $colors {
  .button-#{$color} {
    background: $color;
  }
}
```

This compiles to:

```scss
.button-red {
  background: "red";
}
.button-green {
  background: "green";
}
.button-blue {
  background: "blue";
}
```

Related Tasks:

- Task 21, *Using Lists to Work with Multiple Properties*, on page 56
- Task 25, *Looping Through Maps*, on page 64

23   Manipulating Lists

As well as looping through lists, you can manipulate them by adding new values or joining multiple lists together. Sass provides two functions that can help you with this: *join($list1, $list2, [$separator])* and *append($list1, $val, [$separator])*. Their names are pretty self-explanatory!

join() lets you join together two lists. It simply takes the two lists you pass in, as seen in the example. In that situation, you want to keep the two lists of colors separate for some purposes, but need them to be one large list for others. So, you use join() to merge the two!

append() adds a new item to an existing list. This can help in situations where you need two lists that only have one item that is different. These functions are also useful when creating functions, as you'll see in *Creating Your Own Functions*.

You can pass an optional third argument to both of these functions. The third argument changes the separator used in the output (for example, space or comma).

➤ Join together two lists.

values/join_lists.scss

```scss
$primary-colors: "red", "yellow";
$secondary-colors: "orange", "green";

$all-colors: join($primary-colors, $secondary-colors);

.rainbow {
  background: linear-gradient($all-colors);
}
```

This compiles to:

```scss
.rainbow {
  background: linear-gradient("red", "yellow", "orange", "green");
}
```

➤ Add an item onto a list.

values/append_lists.scss

```scss
$primary-colors: "red", "yellow";

@each $color in append($primary-colors, "blue") {
  .stripe-#{$color} {
    background: $color;
  }
}
```

This compiles to:

```scss
.stripe-red {
  background: "red";
}

.stripe-yellow {
  background: "yellow";
}

.stripe-blue {
  background: "blue";
}
```

Related Tasks:

• Task 21, *Using Lists to Work with Multiple Properties*, on page 56
• Task 26, *Manipulating Maps*, on page 66

24   Using Maps for More Detailed Collections

Maps are a concept from other programming languages with a ton of different names. If you're familiar with programming, you may know them as hashes or dictionaries. They are similar to lists in the sense that they can consist of many items. However, a map has a pair of items. These are known as the *key* and *value*. They're incredibly useful for keeping track of more information than just a list. They keep twice the information and can act almost like collections of variables.

Take a look at the example for this task. There's a map for some flower-themed colors. In the example, the names of the flowers—geranium, daffodil, iris—are the keys of the map. Their associated values are the hex colors. You can reference a key to get a value.

Maps are used in a lot of the same ways as lists, but with some slightly different functions. There's a list of all of them in *Map Functions*, but here you'll learn about a couple of the functions in more detail.

The *map-get($map, $key)* function allows us to find a particular value for a specified key in our map. In our example, we say we want to grab the value for "daffodil" from the $colors map. In our output, we can see that Sass grabs the correct hex value.

Two other useful functions are *map-keys($map)* and *map-values($map)*. These return a list of all the keys or values in the map. See how to use map-values() in the example. All the values—all the hex colors—are being grabbed from the map, then being used to make a gradient.

One other function that's worth mentioning—but that you won't see until a few tasks later—is *map-has-key($map, $key)*. This function returns true or false based on whether the key is present in the map given. So, for the map in the example, map-has-key($colors, geranium) would return true, but map-has-key($colors, daisy) would be false.

➤ Check out this example of a map.

values/maps.scss

```
$colors: (geranium: #B23C56,
          daffodil: #FFF889,
          iris: #45A8CC);
```

➤ Use map functions to grab items from the map.

values/map_functions.scss

```
@import "maps.scss";

.separator {
  background: map-get($colors, daffodil);
}

.rainbow-selector {
  background: linear-gradient(map-values($colors));
}
```

This compiles to:

```
.separator {
  background: #FFF889;
}

.rainbow-selector {
  background: linear-gradient(#B23C56, #FFF889, #45A8CC);
}
```

Related Tasks:

- Task 25, *Looping Through Maps*, on page 64
- Task 26, *Manipulating Maps*, on page 66
- Task 27, *Using Maps for Namespace Configuration*, on page 68

25 Looping Through Maps

You can loop through maps in much the same way you loop through lists. You can use the @each function to go through a map. When looping through maps, much like lists, Sass starts at the beginning of the declaration—so order matters.

When using @each with maps, you have to pass in *two* variables—the key and the value. Here, there's a map that consists of a series of widths of a hero image. These will make the hero image more responsive.

When looping through the $hero-widths, you must create variables for the key (in this case, $size) and the value (in this case, $width). You can then use these variables as necessary. In this case, there's a series of classes that dictate the width of the hero image.

Another handy way to use loops with maps is by creating a header sizes map. You can create a map with keys corresponding to header tags—<h1>, <h2>, and so on. Then, assign font sizes as their values.

➤ Loop through a map.

values/looping_maps.scss

```
$hero-widths: (small: 300px, medium: 600px, large: 900px);
@each $size, $width in $hero-widths {
  .hero-#{$size} {
    width: $width;
  }
}
```

This compiles to:

```
.hero-small {
  width: 300px;
}
.hero-medium {
  width: 600px;
}
.hero-large {
  width: 900px;
}
```

➤ Loop through a map for header sizes.

values/looping_header_maps.scss

```
$typography: (h1: 30px, h2: 22px, h3: 18px);
@each $tag, $size in $typography {
  #{$tag} {
    font-size: $size;
  }
}
```

Related Tasks:

- Task 22, *Looping Through Lists*, on page 58
- Task 24, *Using Maps for More Detailed Collections*, on page 62

26 | Manipulating Maps

As with lists, there are a few ways to edit maps on the fly. The main two functions are *map-merge($map1, $map2)* and *map-remove($map, $keys…)*. Their names are pretty indicative of what they do, but you'll learn about them more here.

map-merge() merges two maps together. Pretty simple, right? In the example, two $social maps are being merged together. This is useful for keeping maps separate in most cases, but needing them to be together for a few occasions. In the example, there's a core set of social colors for the main social brands on the site. However, for icons, *all* the social colors, including some secondary social colors, need to be used. Therefore, map-merge() is used to merge the two maps into one larger map ($all-social).

Unlike with lists, there's no append-style function to add an extra member to a map. Instead, you can use map-merge() and just pass in your additional key-value pair as the second argument. For example, map-merge($social-standard, (gplus: #DD4B39)) would return your $social-standard map with the new key-value appended.

What's important to note about maps is that each key can only appear *once* in a map. Any key that comes later in the map will override any previous keys. This can be dangerous when merging two maps together: any duplicate keys in the second map will obliterate the keys from the first map.

map-remove() takes two arguments—the map from which you want to remove something, and the key for the item you want to remove. This can be useful for one-off occasions where the one item in a map doesn't make sense for a particular situation, so removing it temporarily is convenient.

In the example, there is a list of useful colors paired with the situations in which we use them. It makes sense for notifications, but the info: blue doesn't make sense for buttons. Therefore, another map is created with the info key-value pair removed.

➤ Merge together two maps.

values/join_maps.scss

```
$social-standard: (twitter:  #55ACEE,
                   facebook: #3B5998);
$social-extra: (gplus:    #DD4B39,
                linkedin: #0077B5);

$all-social: map-merge($social-standard, $social-extra);

@each $social, $color in $all-social {
  .#{$social}-icon {
    background: $color;
  }
}
```

This compiles to:

```
.twitter-icon {
  background: #55ACEE;
}

.facebook-icon {
  background: #3B5998;
}

.gplus-icon {
  background: #DD4B39;
}

.linkedin-icon {
  background: #0077B5;
}
```

➤ Remove an item from a map.

values/map_remove.scss

```
$notifications: (confirm: green,
                 error:   red,
                 info: blue);

$button-colors: map-remove($notifications, info);

@each $name, $color in $button-colors {
  .#{$name}-button {
    background: $color;
  }
}
```

Related Tasks:

- Task 23, *Manipulating Lists,* on page 60
- Task 24, *Using Maps for More Detailed Collections,* on page 62

27   Using Maps for Namespace Configuration

As your knowledge of Sass grows, you might want to create your own framework or design system for your team, your company, or maybe even all the web developers out there! A lot of the functions covered in this part would help with that. In particular, maps can help keep a framework from interfering with others' code.

Say you have a color palette you use in your framework. You could define *global* variables, such as $red: #B23C56. But if a user has the same color variable, yours will be overwritten! Not good.

Instead, create a map called, say, $framework-colors. Then, when using the framework colors in your framework, just use the map-get() function.

This may seem like a lot of work, but as you can see in the example, it really helps avoid conflicts when other people use your framework. The user has their own $red variable. If you had used a plain global variable in your framework, you would have caused a conflict with this variable. As you didn't, the framework just works!

You can also create configuration maps for column sizes, headers, and many other features of a framework. In fact, in *Libraries and Frameworks*, you'll learn how this happens in some preexisting frameworks.

➤ Use a map for your framework.

values/map_framework.scss

```scss
$framework-colors: ( red: #B23C56,
                     blue: #44AACC);

@mixin framework-button {
  background: map-get($framework-colors, red)
}
```

➤ Avoid conflicts in variable names.

values/framework_use.scss

```scss
@import "map_framework";

$red: #CC001A;

.normal-button {
  background: $red;
}

.framework-button {
  @include framework-button;
}
```

This compiles to:

```scss
.normal-button {
  background: #CC001A;
}

.framework-button {
  background: #B23C56;
}
```

Related Tasks:

- Task 24, *Using Maps for More Detailed Collections*, on page 62

Part V

Advanced Language Features

Now that you're familiar with most of the basics of Sass, it's time to really dive into the advanced aspects of the language. These aren't necessarily things that you'll use on a day-to-day basis, but they definitely help make Sass the most powerful CSS preprocessor out there.

- First, you'll create your own functions in Task 28, *Creating Your Own Functions*, on page 74.

- In Task 29, *Debugging Your Sass*, on page 76, you'll learn some handy ways to debug your Sass.

- You'll tackle more advanced & usage and BEM syntax in Task 30, *Using & to Implement BEM*, on page 78.

- You'll come across the @extend feature in Task 31, *Using @extend as a Mixin Alternative*, on page 80.

- Then you'll use placeholders in Task 32, *Using Placeholders with @extend*, on page 82.

- You'll learn about some of the issues with @extend in Task 33, *Understanding the Dangers of @extend*, on page 84.

- Finally, you'll use the @at-root function in Task 34, *Escaping Indentation with @root*, on page 86.

28   Creating Your Own Functions

As well as using functions for things such as manipulating lists and maps, and color manipulation, Sass gives you the ability to create your own functions.

Functions are defined similarly to mixins. You define them using the @function directive. Then you can pass in any arguments. Inside the scope of the function, you can perform any number of tasks using standard Sass. The only main difference from a mixin is that you need to use the @return method if you want to make the function return anything.

You can see this in a simple doubling function example. A variable is passed in ($value), and the function returns the variable multiplied by two. When the function is used in the .sidebar class, it outputs 20px rather than 10px.

A more complex example of a function comes from a useful blog post by Hugo Giraudel.[9] In *Using Lists to Work with Multiple Properties*, you learned about the nth function. However, you may often find yourself just grabbing the first or last item on a list. A handy set of functions would be first() and last().

In these functions, shown in the complex example, just the nth() and length() functions are used to grab the necessary indexes needed for the first and last items in a list.

Hugo's blog post has a lot more great functions for manipulation of lists. Check it out!

---

9.   http://hugogiraudel.com/2013/08/08/advanced-sass-list-functions/

➤ Create and use a simple doubling function.

advancedlanguage/simple_function.scss

```
@function double($value) {
  @return $value * 2;
}

$normal-padding: 10px;

.sidebar {
  padding: $normal-padding double($normal-padding);
}
```

This compiles to:

```
.sidebar {
  padding: 10px 20px;
}
```

➤ Create a first and last function for lists.

advancedlanguage/complex_function.scss

```
@function first($list) {
  @return nth($list, 1);
}
@function last($list) {
  @return nth($list, length($list));
}
```

Related Tasks:

• Task 21, *Using Lists to Work with Multiple Properties*, on page 56

29 Debugging Your Sass

Sourcemaps are a feature that allow you to more directly debug your Sass from the browser. Browsers can't "read" Sass—they need it to be compiled into CSS. This means that when you're debugging your site locally, you see only the CSS output rather than the Sass that you've written. Rather than try to figure out which CSS line corresponds to which Sass line, sourcemaps show the exact Sass line in your code.

Sass sourcemaps are enabled by default when you compile your style sheets. When inspecting an element on the page, you can see the Sass file it came from. In the following case, you can see that the <h1> styles that are being implemented come from the _header.scss partial, on line 5.

```
}

header h1 {            _header.scss:5
    font-size: 2em;
}

h1 {           user agent stylesheet
    display: block;
    font-size: 2em;
```

Another useful feature is @*warn*. This function allows you to let others know when there's an error in their code. Take a look at the example. There's a mixin to help with media queries. There's also a map of appropriate screen sizes for our project. The mixin checks that the value ($size) is found in the map. If not, the @warn function is used.

When someone uses the mixin incorrectly—by passing in a breakpoint that isn't present—in the command line, they will see the warning message and the appropriate line number.

➤ advancedlanguage/atwarn.scss

```scss
$breakpoints: (small: 400px,
               medium: 700px,
               large: 1200px);
@mixin larger-than($size) {
  @if map-has-key($breakpoints, $size) {
    @media (min-width: #{map-get($breakpoints, $size)}) {
      @content;
    }
  }
  @else {
    @warn "This is not a valid breakpoint.";
  }
}
////////////////////////////////////////////
.hero-image {
  @include larger-than(extra-large) {
    width: 1400px;
  }
}
```

If you try to compile this Sass, this is generated on the command line:

```
WARNING: This is not a valid breakpoint.
 on line 12 of advancedlanguage/atwarn.scss, in 'larger-than'
 from line 17 of advancedlanguage/atwarn.scss
```

Related Tasks:

- Task 16, *Controlling Flow with @if,* on page 42
- Task 24, *Using Maps for More Detailed Collections,* on page 62

30   Using & to Implement BEM

Back in *Advanced Scoping*, you learned how to use the parent selector to reference all the parent selectors from your current position. However, you can also use the & to modify selectors. This can be especially useful when using BEM style syntax.

BEM (*Block Element Modifier*) is a philosophy for consistent and understandable CSS. It suggests that you treat large pieces of your design as *blocks*. A block has many *elements* inside it, and those elements should have classes that reflect their relationship to their parent. In BEM, this means having the parent name, followed by two underscores, then the element name—as shown in the example with .notification__icon. A *modifier* is an alteration to a block. In the example, that's an alert state that the notification could have. A modifier class is the parent name, plus two dashes, then the modification type—in the example, it's .notification--alert.

You can probably already see a problem with writing this in CSS: you're repeating the .notification part of the class three times! Not very DRY, is it? Thankfully, this is where Sass's parent selector, &, comes in. If you nest your styles within a block selector, you can simply use the & to reference it, then add to the class your extensions on the selector. Check it out in the example. Much easier to read!

You can even use & in mixins to achieve this! You saw how you can use & in *Manipulating @content* to reference the parent selector from within a mixin. You can apply the same principle in order to modify whichever selector you use the mixin on.

In the example, there's a mixin that will modify classes to include an --alert state that has a red background.

➤ Check out some standard BEM syntax.

advancedlanguage/bem.css

```
.notification {
/* This is a block element */
}
.notification__icon {
/* This is a child element of the block */
}
.notification--alert {
/* This is a different state of the block */
}
```

➤ Use & to make code more DRY.

advancedlanguage/ampersand_bem.scss

```
.notification {
  padding: 20px;
  &__icon {
    margin: 10px 20px;  } }
```

This compiles to:

```
.notification {
  padding: 20px;
}
.notification__icon {
  margin: 10px 20px;
}
```

➤ Make a mixin with &.

advancedlanguage/ampersand_mixin.scss

```
@mixin add_alert_modifier {
  &--alert {
    background: red; } }

.notification {
  @include add_alert_modifier;
}
```

This compiles to:

```
.notification--alert {
  background: red; }
```

Related Tasks:

- Task 4, *Advanced Scoping,* on page 10

31   Using @extend as a Mixin Alternative

In *Keeping Code Clean with Mixins*, you learned about mixins—ways to apply one set of styles to another area of your code. There's another way to achieve a similar outcome, and that's by using *@extend*.

The @extend function *extends* any styles from a previous selector onto a new selector. So, say you had a .button class. You may want to copy those styles over to a different type of button. Just use @extend .button; in the new class and it works!

You might be wondering why you would use the @extend> function rather than a mixin. Don't they just do the same thing? Well, not really. You'll discover more of the differences in *Understanding the Dangers of @extend*, but for now, here's the most obvious: duplication of code.

When you @include a mixin, the CSS written in the mixin is included under the new selector. If you use the mixin in a second selector, that CSS is repeated in that selector. Extends copy your *selector* over to the original selector.

This copying can be seen in the example. @extend is used on two other buttons to duplicate the styles from the original button class. Those other selectors are then chained to the original selector in the output.

➤ Use @extend to copy over classes.

advancedlanguage/atextend.scss

```scss
.button {
  border-radius: 2px;
  padding: 10px 20px;
  text-transform: capitalize;
}
.button-register {
  @extend .button;
  background: green;
}
.button-cancel {
  @extend .button;
  background: red;
}
```

This compiles to:

```css
.button, .button-register, .button-cancel {
  border-radius: 2px;
  padding: 10px 20px;
  text-transform: capitalize;
}
.button-register {
  background: green;
}
.button-cancel {
  background: red;
}
```

Related Tasks:

- Task 8, *Keeping Code Clean with Mixins,* on page 18
- Task 32, *Using Placeholders with @extend,* on page 82
- Task 33, *Understanding the Dangers of @extend,* on page 84

32 Using Placeholders with @extend

In the previous task, you learned about @extend. It was used to extend a .button class. Those styles were applied to two new classes, which could then be used in some markup. But you don't really need the .button selector as it's too generic. It's only being used to extend its style rules onto other selectors.

This is where *placeholders* come in. You can define a placeholder by using the % sign. Then, you declare your styles as usual, and you can extend the styles to other classes as seen in the example.

On compilation, though, *placeholders are omitted* from the final output. In the example, this means that the %button placeholder selector is not present in the output. This keeps your final CSS cleaner.

At this point, an interesting question arises: if neither mixins nor placeholders are compiled into your CSS, when should you use a mixin and when should you use extend?

Many people only use mixins when there needs to be some variation in the code—for example, only use a mixin when you need to pass in arguments. If the declaration block is going to be exactly the same, use @extend as this doesn't duplicate your styles every time.

➤ Extend a placeholder rather than a selector.

advancedlanguage/atextend_placeholder.scss

```
%button {
  border-radius: 2px;
  padding: 10px 20px;
  text-transform: capitalize;
}

.button-register {
  @extend %button;
  background: green;
}

.button-cancel {
  @extend %button;
  background: red;
}
```

This compiles to:

```
.button-register, .button-cancel {
  border-radius: 2px;
  padding: 10px 20px;
  text-transform: capitalize;
}

.button-register {
  background: green;
}

.button-cancel {
  background: red;
}
```

Related Tasks:

- Task 31, *Using @extend as a Mixin Alternative,* on page 80

33 Understanding the Dangers of @extend

@extend is certainly powerful, but it can cause bloated output styles if not used carefully.

The example illustrates how just a couple of @extend uses can quickly spiral into some bloated output. All that's happening is that the .small-icon class is extended onto two other areas. However, where it's being extended is a little messy. There's a couple of nested selectors, and they use commas. So Sass has to add all of those class permutations onto the original class, which leaves us with the bloated output you see.

This example shouldn't suggest that you should never use @extend. Instead, it should illustrate that when choosing between a mixin or extend, you need to think about how you might be using it. It also shows that you should think about your selectors and try to keep them simple if possible.

Another important aspect to note is that a selector cannot be extended from a media query. This is because the intention isn't clear. Do you want the whole selector including the media query, or just the non-media query selectors? Sass will therefore throw an error if you try to extend from within media queries.

➤ Extend a seemingly innocent selector.

advancedlanguage/atextend_messy.scss

```scss
.button .interior .small-icon {
 width: 10px;
}
.side {
 .top, .middle, .bottom {
   .sign-in, .register {
     @extend .small-icon;
   }
 }
}
.footer {
 .links, .social {
   .facebook, .twitter {
     @extend .small-icon;
   }
 }
}
```

This compiles to:

```css
.button .interior .small-icon, .button .interior .side .top
.sign-in, .side .top .button .interior .sign-in, .button
.interior .side .top .register, .side .top .button .interior
.register, .button .interior .side .middle .sign-in, .side
.middle .button .interior .sign-in, .button .interior .side
.middle .register, .side .middle .button .interior .register,
.button .interior .side .bottom .sign-in, .side .bottom
.button .interior .sign-in, .button .interior .side .bottom
.register, .side .bottom .button .interior .register, .button
.interior .footer .links .facebook, .footer .links .button
.interior .facebook, .button .interior .footer .links
.twitter, .footer .links .button .interior .twitter, .button
.interior .footer .social .facebook, .footer .social .button
.interior .facebook, .button .interior .footer .social
.twitter, .footer .social .button .interior .twitter {
  width: 10px; }
```

Related Tasks:

- Task 31, *Using @extend as a Mixin Alternative,* on page 80

34   Escaping Indentation with @root

Sometimes, for code clarity, we want to keep our styles close together. And this might mean that we're in the middle of a nested block of Sass when we really want to be outside of it. This is where @at-root comes in handy.

In our example, we have a header icon we want to style. It's mainly found in the header, so we want to associate the icon with those styles. However, we might want to use the icon elsewhere, so we'd really like the styles to be more global. We use @at-root to *flatten* the nesting and make .icon at the root of the document.

There aren't a lot of use cases for @at-root—moderating our nesting is an equally appropriate solution. However, there are a couple of situations that people have found it to be useful.

In our second example, we use @at-root with interpolation. On many sites, we use a button class on some links to make them stand out more and encourage users to click them. However, resetting an <a> tag requires us to add an extra rule—text-decoration: none. Rather than apply this to *every* button, we only apply it to an <a> tag with the button class. Keeping it inside the button declaration block makes it easier for us to find our code later on.

Another handy way to use @at-root is to escape a media query. If we use the code (without: media), we can escape any media queries that we were inside. We can also use @at-root to help us write BEM-style selectors, as described in a great blog post by Una Kravets.[10]

---

10.   http://una.im/2013/10/15/sass-3-3-at-root-bem/

➤ Use @at-root to escape nesting.

advancedlanguage/atroot.scss

```scss
header {
  .menu {
    float: right;
    @at-root .icon {
      border-radius: 50%;
      height: 10px;
      width: 10px;
    }
  }
}
```

This compiles to:

```scss
header .menu {
  float: right;
}
.icon {
  border-radius: 50%;
  height: 10px;
  width: 10px;
}
```

➤ Escape and interpolate with @at-root.

advancedlanguage/atroot_buttonlink.scss

```scss
.button {
  border-radius: 2px;
  min-width: 200px;
  padding: 10px 20px;
  @at-root a#{&} {
    text-decoration: none;
  }
}
```

This compiles to:

```scss
.button {
  border-radius: 2px;
  min-width: 200px;
  padding: 10px 20px;
}
a.button {
  text-decoration: none;
}
```

Part VI

Libraries and Frameworks

Writing your own Sass is fun, and with all the knowledge you've learned so far, you can definitely write some efficient, easy-to-read style sheets. However, you can go the extra mile by using frameworks and libraries.

You'll explore some of the more popular frameworks for Sass in this part.

What's important to note is that some Sass libraries can only be used with Ruby projects—due to Sass historically having to be compiled with Ruby. If your project isn't Ruby-based, those types of libraries aren't going to be a good fit. That's something to keep in mind throughout this part and when thinking about libraries and frameworks in general.

- You'll learn about frameworks that do a lot of things in Task 35, *Fully Featured Frameworks*, on page 92.

- Then, you'll take a deeper dive into a layout library in Task 36, *Using Grid Systems for Layout*, on page 94.

- In Task 37, *Introducing Eyeglass*, on page 96, you'll use the npm-based dependency management system, Eyeglass.

- Then, you'll explore two ways to use Eyeglass in Task 38, *Doing Math with Eyeglass*, on page 98, and Task 39, *Spriting with Eyeglass*, on page 100.

35   Fully Featured Frameworks

Frameworks and libraries are collections of mixins and functions that help us with our style sheets. There are hundreds of them out there, and choosing one is often dependent on the specific needs of a project.

Bourbon[11] is one example of a lightweight Sass library. It comes with a number of features that can be useful in a project. In particular, a lot of its mixins take care of the cross-browser compatibility issues we saw in *Using Mixins for Cross-Browser Compatibility*. Rather than writing all our own mixins to take care of cross-browser quirks, we can take advantage of Bourbon's collection of mixins.

As well as mixins, there are some useful functions present, too. For example, the em() method converts a pixel value into an em value (using 16px as a base). In our example, we use one of Bourbon's mixins and one function to illustrate how it works.

Bourbon is just one example of a Sass library. There are many more out there with similar features. Some are simpler, and some have more complex assets. Pick which one is right for you!

The downside of using a library can be the lack of flexibility associated with it. Libraries often come with their own color scheme, which could make our site look generic. Most libraries do allow for some customization, but that can sometimes be more of a headache than just coding our own styles to begin with.

---

11.   http://bourbon.io/

➤ Install Bourbon with Ruby.

```
gem install bourbon
bourbon install
```

➤ Install Bourbon with npm.

```
npm install --save bourbon
```

➤ Use some of Bourbon's features.

frameworks/bourbon.scss

```scss
@import "bourbon/bourbon";

.hero-text {
  @include transform(rotate(90deg));
  font-size: em(20);
}
```

This compiles to:

```css
.hero-text {
  -webkit-transform: rotate(90deg);
  -moz-transform: rotate(90deg);
  -ms-transform: rotate(90deg);
  -o-transform: rotate(90deg);
  transform: rotate(90deg);
  font-size: 1.25em; }
```

Related Tasks:

- Task 36, *Using Grid Systems for Layout,* on page 94
- Task 37, *Introducing Eyeglass,* on page 96

36 Using Grid Systems for Layout

One of the more complex situations to deal with when implementing styles on a site is even grid spacing—especially implementing the regular spacing found on a Photoshop design.

Grids should be flexible and are usually percentage-based. They also dictate *gutters*. Gutters are how wide you want the spaces in between your columns to be.

Implementing a grid can be tricky. How much space should you leave for margins? What *exact* percentages should you use? There are a number of frameworks to help with these issues.

Bourbon Neat[12] is a grid framework that builds on Bourbon. To use Neat, you have to install Bourbon first (as introduced in *Fully Featured Frameworks*). Then, you can install Neat in a similar way, as shown:

```
gem install neat
neat install
```

You must have @import "neat/neat"; at the top of your style sheet, and then you're ready to go.

You can use the mixins provided by Neat to create your grid system. On a wrapper (.profile), you use the outer-container mixin, as shown in the example.

Then you can use the span-columns mixin to assign how wide you want each column to be. Neat, by default, has a twelve-column grid—although this can be changed if necessary. To span 100% of the width, you make .information eight columns wide and .photos four columns wide. It's that simple!

The output from Neat is quite extensive—you can see why it's preferable to use a framework like this rather than cover all the edge cases yourself!

Having a grid system dictate all the sizes we need can be at odds with our intended design. This is where another grid system, Susy,[13] is worth looking at. Susy has a complex math back end to make creating grid systems easy. If you need more control over your grid system, consider using Susy.

---

12. http://neat.bourbon.io/
13. http://susy.oddbird.net/

➤ Use Neat's mixins to make a grid.

frameworks/bourbon_neat.scss

```scss
@import "bourbon/bourbon";
@import "neat/neat";

.profile {
  @include outer-container;
  .information {
    @include span-columns(8);
  }
  .photos {
    @include span-columns(4); } }
```

This compiles to:

```css
html {
  box-sizing: border-box; }

*, *::after, *::before {
  box-sizing: inherit; }

.profile {
  max-width: 68em;
  margin-left: auto;
  margin-right: auto; }
.profile::after {
  clear: both;
  content: "";
  display: table; }
.profile .information {
  float: left;
  display: block;
  margin-right: 2.35765%;
  width: 65.88078%; }
.profile .information:last-child {
  margin-right: 0; }
.profile .photos {
  float: left;
  display: block;
  margin-right: 2.35765%;
  width: 31.76157%; }
.profile .photos:last-child {
  margin-right: 0; }
```

Related Tasks:

- Task 35, *Fully Featured Frameworks*, on page 92

37   Introducing Eyeglass

Eyeglass is a modular dependency-management system that allows you to use some of the thousands of packages available for Sass. These packages mean that you can add functionality to your style sheets, making it simple to manage, install, and discover better libraries that you can use in your Sass code.

For example, if you want to use some timer functions of Eyeglass, you install the eyeglass-timer module into your project. This modular system keeps your projects much cleaner.

Eyeglass is npm-based, which means that any project using npm can easily install Eyeglass. In the example, you can see how to do that. broccoli-eyeglass is the recommended way to use Eyeglass and its modules.

Once broccoli-eyeglass is installed, you can set up a simple Brocfile.js and write some JavaScript to help you compile your Sass. There are opportunities to say where to place output (css in the example), as well as indicate where the Sass files are (in the src folder in the example). When building the project, you run the command in the example, which puts the output css folder into a folder called assets. If there are any Sass files in the src folder, they will be compiled and outputted by Broccoli. Simple!

Installing further modules is easy—just use npm install with the name of the module. The module will be added to the package.json file, then you're free to use all its features in your Sass.

The list of official Eyeglass npm packages can be found on the Eyeglass GitHub page,[14] and even more can be found by searching for Eyeglass on the npm packages site.[15]

---

14.   https://github.com/sass-eyeglass
15.   https://www.npmjs.com/search?q=eyeglass

➤ Install Broccoli and Eyeglass.

```
npm install broccoli --save-dev
npm install broccoli-cli --global
npm install broccoli-eyeglass --save-dev
```

➤ Use a simple Brocfile.js.

frameworks/brocfile.js

```
var BroccoliEyeglass = require('broccoli-eyeglass');

var options = {
  cssDir: "css"
}
var outputTree = new BroccoliEyeglass(["src"], options);

module.exports = outputTree;
```

➤ Build a project with Broccoli.

```
broccoli build assets
```

Related Tasks:

- Task 38, *Doing Math with Eyeglass*, on page 98
- Task 39, *Spriting with Eyeglass*, on page 100

38   Doing Math with Eyeglass

Creating shapes, perfecting animations, or making canvases can all require some complex mathematical functions. Sass includes some basic operators, but for more in-depth functionality, you should turn to the eyeglass-math module.

Once you've installed the module using the command in the example, you need to use @import "math"; in your style sheet to include all the math functions.

In the first example, the $PI variable and the sqrt() function are used to calculate the diameter of a circle. This could be useful for generating CSS circles with areas that are tied to specific values.

You can calculate heights and widths of triangles using trigonometric functions. eyeglass-math comes with all the major trigonometry functions, including sin(), cos(), and tan().

In the rectangle example, the pow() function is used to calculate 2 to the power of 4, then the cbrt() function to calculate a cube root.

As well as $PI, there are other constants: $TAU and $E. You can find a list of all the other functions on the GitHub page for eyeglass-math.[16]

---

16. https://github.com/sass-eyeglass/eyeglass-math

➤ Install Eyeglass math.

```
npm install eyeglass-math --save
```

➤ Use complex math functions.

frameworks/eyeglass_math.scss

```scss
@import "math";

$radius: sqrt(250/$PI);
$diameter: (2px * $radius);
.circle {
  border-radius: 50%;
  height: $diameter;
  width: $diameter;
}

$hypotenuse: 300px;
.triangle {
  height: 20px;
  width: (sin(40)*$hypotenuse);
}

.rectangle {
  height: pow(2, 4);
  width: cbrt(216);
}
```

This compiles to:

```css
.circle {
  border-radius: 50%;
  height: 17.84124px;
  width: 17.84124px;
}
.triangle {
  height: 20px;
  width: 223.53395px;
}
.rectangle {
  height: 16;
  width: 6;
}
```

Related Tasks:

- Task 37, *Introducing Eyeglass,* on page 96

39 Spriting with Eyeglass

Spriting is a process by which many small icons or pictures are turned into one larger one for use in a website. The one larger file is not the direct sum of its parts—its file size is a lot smaller than the separate images combined. This is of supreme importance in the age of the mobile web, where every KB counts.

There's a special Eyeglass module for spriting images. In a project, just install it using the command seen in the example.

Once the module has installed, you can import the spriting module in your Sass file—which you can see in the example. As images are being used, you need to instruct Eyeglass to be ready to handle assets. You do that by importing "assets".

You can then tell Eyeglass to create a map of sprites. You should create a variable to store them in (for example, $button-icons), then use the sprite-map() function to prepare it. You then pass in the name of the map, followed by the style of sprite file you want to create, then finally a link to the folder where you're keeping your sprite images.

When you want to use a sprite, you should include three mixins: sprite-background, sprite-position, and sprite-dimensions. You only need to pass in a reference to the map and, in the case of the latter two, a reference to the icon you want (which is the path to your file). You can see this in the example.

It's also easy to loop over the sprite map and generate a bunch of classes with appropriate backgrounds. Use @each to loop through the map, then create a class using interpolation. Then just assign the same three mixins to the class.

➤ Install eyeglass-spriting.

```
npm install eyeglass-spriting --save-dev
```

➤ Use Eyeglass to sprite images.

frameworks/spriting.scss

```
@import "spriting";
@import "assets";

$button-icons: sprite-map("button-icons",
                    sprite-layout(horizontal, (spacing: 5px,
                                                alignment: bottom)),
                    "images/icons/*");)
.alert-icon {
  @include sprite-background($button-icons);
  @include sprite-position($button-icons, "images/icons/alert.png");
  @include sprite-dimensions($button-icons, "images/icons/alert.png");
}
```

➤ Create a number of classes with icon backgrounds.

frameworks/spriting_loop.scss

```
@each $icon in sprite-list($button-icons) {
  .#{sprite-identifier($button-icons, $icon)}-icon {
    @include sprite-background($button-icons);
    @include sprite-position($button-icons, $icon);
    @include sprite-dimensions($button-icons, $icon);
  }
}
```

Related Tasks:

• Task 37, *Introducing Eyeglass,* on page 96

SassScript Function Reference

The following function reference comes from the Sass documentation, with some alterations for clarity. If a variable is in square brackets, that means it's optional.

RGB Functions

rgb($red, $green, $blue)

Creates a new color from red, green, and blue values.

rgba($red, $green, $blue, $alpha)

Creates a new color from red, green, blue, and alpha (opacity) values.

red($color)

Gets the red component of a color.

green($color)

Gets the green component of a color.

blue($color)

Gets the blue component of a color.

mix($color1, $color2, [$weight])

Mixes two colors together. More specifically, it takes the averages of the RGB components, weighted by the optional $weight value. The default value for $weight is 50%—for example, 50% of the first color and 50% of the second color.

HSL Functions

hsl($hue, $saturation, $lightness)

Creates a color from hue, saturation, and lightness values.

hsla($hue, $saturation, $lightness, $alpha)

Creates a color from hue, saturation, lightness, and alpha (opacity) values.

hue($color)

Gets the hue component of a color.

saturation($color)

Gets the saturation component of a color.

lightness($color)

Gets the lightness component of a color.

adjust-hue($color, $degrees)

Changes the hue of a color, maintaining the lightness and saturation. The degrees given rotate the hue.

lighten($color, $amount)

Makes a color lighter. The amount is given in a percentage.

darken($color, $amount)

Makes a color darker. The amount is given in a percentage.

saturate($color, $amount)

Makes a color more saturated. The amount is given in a percentage.

desaturate($color, $amount)

Makes a color less saturated. The amount is given in a percentage.

grayscale($color)

Converts a color to grayscale. Essentially, this is the same as using desaturate($color, 100%).

complement($color)

Returns the complement of a color.

invert($color)

Returns the inverse of a color.

Opacity Functions

alpha($color) / opacity($color)

Gets the alpha component (opacity) of a color.

rgba($color, $alpha)

Changes the alpha (opacity) component for a color.

opacify($color, $amount) / fade-in($color, $amount)

Makes a color more opaque. The $amount value should be between 0 and 1.

transparentize($color, $amount) / fade-out($color, $amount)

Makes a color more transparent. The $amount value should be between 0 and 1.

Other Color Functions

adjust-color($color, [$red], [$green], [$blue], [$hue], [$saturation], [$lightness], [$alpha])

Increases or decreases one or more components of a color. The color variables should be between 0 and 255 in value.

scale-color($color, [$red], [$green], [$blue], [$saturation], [$lightness], [$alpha])

Fluidly scales one or more properties of a color.

change-color($color, [$red], [$green], [$blue], [$hue], [$saturation], [$lightness], [$alpha])

Changes one or more properties of a color to the value specified.

ie-hex-str($color)

Converts a color into the format understood by IE filters.

String Functions

unquote($string)

Removes quotes from a string.

quote($string)

Adds quotes to a string.

str-length($string)

Returns the number of characters in a string.

str-insert($string, $insert, $index)

Inserts $insert into $string at $index.

str-index($string, $substring)

Returns the index of the first occurrence of the $substring in the $string specified.

str-slice($string, $start-at, [$end-at])

Extracts a substring from $string.

to-upper-case($string)

Converts a string to uppercase.

to-lower-case($string)

Converts a string to lowercase.

Number Functions

percentage($number)

Converts a unitless number to a percentage.

round($number)

Rounds a number to the nearest whole number.

ceil($number)

Rounds a number up to the next whole number.

floor($number)

Rounds a number down to the previous whole number.

abs($number)

Returns the absolute value of a number.

min($numbers...)

Finds the minimum of several numbers.

max($numbers...)

Finds the maximum of several numbers.

random([$limit])

Returns a random number. $limit defines the top number from which Sass will pick the random number.

List Functions

Lists in Sass are immutable; all list functions return a new list rather than updating the existing list in place.

All list functions work for maps as well, treating them as lists of pairs. For example, the map (register: green, sign-out: red) would be treated as ((register, green), (sign-out, red)).

length($list)

Returns the length of a list.

nth($list, $n)

Returns a specific item in a list.

set-nth($list, $n, $value)

Replaces the nth item in a list.

join($list1, $list2, [$separator])

Joins together two lists into one.

append($list1, $val, [$separator])

Appends a single value onto the end of a list.

zip($lists...)

Combines several lists into a single multidimensional list.

index($list, $value)

Returns the position of a value within a list.

list-separator($list)

Returns the separator of a list.

Map Functions

Maps in Sass are immutable; all map functions return a new map rather than updating the existing map in place.

map-get($map, $key)

Returns the value in a map associated with a given key.

map-merge($map1, $map2)

Merges two maps together into a new map.

map-remove($map, $keys...)

Returns a new map with keys removed.

map-keys($map)

Returns a list of all keys in a map.

map-values($map)

Returns a list of all values in a map.

map-has-key($map, $key)

Returns if a map has a value associated with a given key.

keywords($args)

Returns the keywords passed to a function that takes variable arguments.

Selector Functions

Selector functions are liberal in the formats they support for selector arguments. They can take a plain string, a list of lists as returned by &, or anything in between:

A plain string, such as ".foo .bar, .baz .bang".

A space-separated list of strings such as (".foo" ".bar").

A comma-separated list of strings such as (".foo .bar", ".baz .bang").

A comma-separated list of space-separated lists of strings such as ((".foo" ".bar"), (".baz" ".bang")).

In general, selector functions allow placeholder selectors (such as %foo) but ban parent-reference selectors (such as &).

selector-nest($selectors...)

Nests selectors beneath one another like they would be nested in the style sheet.

selector-append($selectors...)

Appends selectors to one another without spaces in between.

selector-extend($selector, $extendee, $extender)

Extends $extendee with $extender within $selector.

selector-replace($selector, $original, $replacement)

Replaces $original with $replacement within $selector.

selector-unify($selector1, $selector2)

Unifies two selectors to produce a selector that matches elements matched by both.

is-superselector($super, $sub)

Returns whether $super matches all the elements $sub does, and possibly more.

simple-selectors($selector)

Returns the simple selectors that comprise a compound selector.

selector-parse($selector)

Parses a selector into the format returned by &.

Introspection Functions

feature-exists($feature)

Returns whether a feature exists in the current Sass runtime.

variable-exists($name)

Returns whether a variable with the given name exists in the current scope.

global-variable-exists($name)

Returns whether a variable with the given name exists in the global scope.

function-exists($name)

Returns whether a function with the given name exists.

mixin-exists($name)

Returns whether a mixin with the given name exists.

inspect($value)

Returns the string representation of a value as it would be represented in Sass.

type-of($value)

Returns the type of a value.

unit($number)

Returns the unit(s) associated with a number.

unitless($number)

Returns whether a number has units.

comparable($number1, $number2)

Returns whether two numbers can be added, subtracted, or compared.

call($name, $args...)

Dynamically calls a Sass function.

Other Functions

if($condition, $if-true, $if-false)

Returns one of two values, depending on whether or not $condition is true.

unique-id()

Returns a unique CSS identifier.

APPENDIX 2

Introduction to Haml

Haml is something of a sister language to Sass, but Haml
was actually designed before Sass. It was successful enough
that a CSS version was developed, applying the same prin-
ciples of Haml into CSS. They were both developed to clarify
the meaning behind design.

Haml was created from the desire to write logically structured HTML that your designer would thank you for. HTML
builders shouldn't make crap: the layout of the page and
the information on the page should be logically structured
and well named. Haml isn't a revolution; it's a statement of
the obvious and an adoption of best practices.

Installing Haml is pretty similar to installing Sass. Once
Ruby is installed, all you need to type in the command line
is the following:

```
gem install haml
```

And you're done. It used to be that Haml was in the same
gem as Sass, but since version 3.1, they've been split into
two separate gems.

If you need any help with Haml, there's the Haml site and
all its documentation,[1] which will have a lot more information than the snippet we've given here. In addition, there's
a bunch of friendly people willing to help at the Haml
Google group.[2]

---

1. http://haml.info/ and http://haml.info/docs/yardoc/file.REFERENCE.html,
respectively.
2. http://groups.google.com/group/haml

In this appendix, we've got two ways to take you through Haml. The first is from a Ruby-style angle, taking an example of ERB and reformatting it. The second is for those of us who are more familiar with HTML. They're both in a slightly different format to the rest of the book, as they follow the progression of ERB/HTML into Haml.

Haml Walkthrough: ERB

Now we're going to walk you through the exact same process with which Haml was created. A well-formatted bit of HTML was changed step by step until Haml was born.

Let's start with an example using ERB. It's a standard template you might find in any Ruby project. Don't panic if you aren't a Rubyist—it's a straightforward example.

haml/haml_e1.html
```
<div id="products">
  <%- @products.each do |product| %>
    <div class="product" id="product_<%= product.id %>">
      <div class="name"><%= product.name %></div>
      <div class="price"><%= product.price %></div>
    </div>
  <% end %>
</div>
```

Executing this would print out each of the products in @products and assign each one a custom ID like product_23 (where the product's ID is 23). It's a standard and well-formatted kind of template in ERB, and we're going to slowly convert this into Haml.

First off: it's important to correctly indent ERB files, so there's no reason why you should have to spend so much time closing tags—it just seems wasteful. So, we'll take the previous example and remove all of the closing tags.

haml/haml_e2.html
```
<div id="products">
  <%- @products.each do |product| %>
    <div class="product" id="product_<%= product.id %>">
      <div class="name"><%= product.name %>
      <div class="price"><%= product.price %>
```

See how much cleaner it is? And notice that the <% end %> tag is gone too. Haml automatically figures out when to close a Ruby block. (This can vary in non-Ruby implementations.)

You're probably thinking we're secretly Python people because of the decision to make Haml "whitespace sensitive." That term's annoying. When looking at HTML, the advantages of getting rid of the closing tags are clear. Even when working in a language that doesn't care about whitespace, most people still do. Having bad indentation is a serious issue in any code or markup and should be treated as a flaw.

Haml used to accept only two spaces as indentation—no exceptions. That has since changed. Whatever you use to start indenting is what you must keep with. Just stay consistent. It can be a tab, or one space, or two tabs. It doesn't matter. As long as it's consistent, it's OK.[3]

Moving on! We're not nearly done yet.

Don't you absolutely hate this line?

```
id="product_<%= product.id %>"
```

Ruby has a fantastic built-in string interpolation feature that means you should be able to do product_#{product.id} and skip all that weirdness. So let's do that.

haml/haml_e3.html

```
<div id="products">
  <%- @products.each do |product| %>
    <div class="product" id="product_#{product.id}">
      <div class="name"><%= product.name %>
      <div class="price"><%= product.price %>
```

There's only a small change this time, but already this example is far more readable. Always think about how readable something is at a glance. When you look at it, how quickly does your brain parse and understand what you're seeing? Basically, this removes a bunch of unneeded symbols for your eyes to deal with.

---

3. However, we're still of the belief that using two spaces is far superior and should be used in Haml. We were convinced by an article by Jamie Zawinski that we strongly suggest you read: http://www.jwz.org/doc/tabs-vs-spaces.html

It's at this point that everyone's dislike of % style tags comes to full vengeance. Has anyone else done PHP for too many years and been left scarred and angry? Let's get rid of those!

haml/haml_e4.html

```
<div id="products">
  - @products.each do |product|
    <div class="product" id="product_#{product.id}">
      <div class="name">
        = product.name
      <div class="price">
        = product.price
```

See, we kept the first character as - or = to signify nonprinting and printing lines. Anything after an = gets printed, and anything after a - is executed but its output ignored.

At this point in the transformation, printing lines have been moved down to their own line. We'll actually rectify this later, but for now it makes parsing the document a lot easier. Besides, <div>= seems inelegant for some reason.

In order to get those back up on the other line, Haml tags must be different from static HTML tags. One of the design goals is that you can copy in some plain HTML (properly indented) and it won't get too mad at you. Mostly this was a concern for the <meta> tags on a page, which no matter what you do are as ugly as sin.

So, let's use the % character to mean <tag> and use the Ruby/JSON-style syntax for the attributes. (Note: the JSON-style syntax only works with Ruby versions 1.9+. In 1.8, you must use the hash rocket style of {"class" => "product"}.)

haml/haml_e5.html

```
%div{id: "products"}
  - @products.each do |product|
    %div{class: "product" id: "product_#{product.id}"}
      %div{class: "name"}
        = product.name
      %div{class: "price"}
        = product.price
```

At this point, we have fully valid Haml. Congratulations! But we have a bit more to do. With this, we can now move those printing lines up again! It'll look nice.

haml/haml_e6.html

```
%div{id: "products"}
  - @products.each do |product|
    %div{class: "product" id: "product_#{product.id}"}
      %div{class: "name"}= product.name
      %div{class: "price"}= product.price
```

Now we're getting somewhere! But something is still not quite right. There's a lot of writing of class: and id:, and it requires the brain to read the letters to understand what it means. At this point, inspiration strikes. Can you think of a symbology that already exists for IDs and classes?

haml/haml_e7.html

```
%div#products
  - @products.each do |product|
    %div.product{id: "product_#{product.id}"}
      %div.name= product.name
      %div.price= product.price
```

Bam! Using CSS-style naming! We already know what those symbols mean. We're on a roll now!

In a larger example, there would be %div all over the place. And we still aren't encouraging the use of classes and IDs. It's a *lot* easier—a lot less typing to do the right thing.

What if we assumed that each tag was a <div> by default?

haml/haml_e8.html

```
#products
  - @products.each do |product|
    .product{id: "product_#{product.id}"}
      .name= product.name
      .price= product.price
```

Now that's nice! We only have to specify the name when it's not a <div>. And if we're lazy, it's easier to name <div>s well than it is to type %div over and over again. This is precisely how Haml should encourage good behavior. With this shortcut, it's hard to do the wrong thing and easier to do the right thing (in other words, name everything well!).

Now we've arrived at some standard Haml. But there's one thing that is still troublesome—the whole id: "product_#{product.id}" line. It's a bit of an ugly duckling there.

If our object has a good answer for the object.id call, then we can automatically figure out the ID and class name that the .product <div> should have. We take the object's class and down-case it, add an underscore, then put in the obj.id value.

haml/haml_e9.haml

```
#products
  - @products.each do |product|
    %div[product]
      .name=  product.name
      .price= product.price
```

The .product <div> will automatically receive the proper class and ID, as in our .product example. When we say [product], though, we're referring to the |product| variable. If we had named the variable in |product| as |x|, then it would be %div[x].

Haml Walkthrough: HTML

We're not going to go through the HTML-to-Haml conversion in detail like the previous ERB one. We just want to see how the stylistic changes can also be applied to a static site.

haml/haml_h1.html

```
<!DOCTYPE html PUBLIC "-//W3C//DTD XHTML 1.0
Transitional//EN" "http://www.w3.org/TR/xhtml1/DTD/
xhtml1-transitional.dtd">
<html xmlns="http://www.w3.org/1999/xhtml"
xml:lang="en">
  <head>
    <meta http-equiv="Content-Type" content="text/html;
charset=UTF-8" />
    <title><%= @title || "Awesome Site" %></title>
  </head>
  <body>
    <div id='wrapper'>
      <div id='header'>
        <h1>Awesome Site</h1>
      </div>
      <div id='content'>
        <%= yield %>
      </div>
      <div id='footer'>
        <small>Copyright Hampton Lintorn Catlin</small>
      </div>
    </div>
  </body>
</html>
```

Pretty standard stuff. In this example (à la Rails), the yield part is where we print out the page-specific contents. Let's convert it the way that we know how so far.

Note: try doing these next few steps along with us. Grab one of your sites, throw it into a tmp file, and start hacking away at it. We promise it feels great!

First thing's first: rip out those pesky end tags!

haml/haml_h2.html

```
<!DOCTYPE html PUBLIC "-//W3C//DTD XHTML 1.0
Transitional//EN" "http://www.w3.org/TR/xhtml1/DTD/
xhtml1-transitional.dtd">
<html xmlns="http://www.w3.org/1999/xhtml"
xml:lang="en">
 <head>
   <meta http-equiv="Content-Type" content="text/html;
charset=UTF-8" />
   <title><%= @title || "Awesome Site" %>
 <body>
   <div id='wrapper'>
     <div id='header'>
       <h1>Awesome Site
     <div id='content'>
       <%= yield %>
     <div id='footer'>
       <small>Copyright Hampton Lintorn Catlin
```

Much neater. Let's Hamlize it even more! Go ahead and get rid of the <div> tags too. No sense in wasting our time.

Note: for the HTML tag, we have to use the old-school hash rocket syntax for Ruby attributes. Why? Because the JSON-style attributes don't allow dashes in them. Stupid Ruby hashes.

haml/haml_h3.html

```
<!DOCTYPE html PUBLIC "-//W3C//DTD XHTML 1.0
Transitional//EN" "http://www.w3.org/TR/xhtml1/DTD/
xhtml1-transitional.dtd">
%html{'xmlns' => "http://www.w3.org/1999/xhtml",
'xml:lang' => "en"}
 %head
   <meta http-equiv="Content-Type" content="text/html;
charset=UTF-8" />
   %title= @title || "Awesome Site"
 %body
   #wrapper
```

```
#header
  %h1 Awesome Site
#content= yield
#footer
  %small Copyright Hampton Lintorn Catlin
```

A few things to notice: when the contents aren't dynamic, you can just put them after the tag name. For instance: %small Copyright Hampton Lintorn Catlin. No equals sign means it's not going to evaluate it: it's just static text.

Also, we left the meta tag alone. It's ugly and will remain ugly. Converting it to a Haml tag achieves nothing. So normally we have to leave that, but for your reference, here is how to do a self-closing tag like that:

```
%meta{"http-equiv" => "Content-Type", "content" =>
  "text/html; charset=UTF-8"}/
```

We just put a / on the end, and the tag knows to self-close. So if we wanted to write <br/>, we could write %br/ instead.

We still have one really ugly thing left on this page—the DOCTYPE! Ugh. How many people just copy and paste from one project to another? We definitely do! So in Haml, we have a lovely little helper (named after one of our favorite bands) called !!! that does the job for us.

haml/haml_h4.html

```
!!!
%html{'xmlns' => "http://www.w3.org/1999/xhtml",
'xml:lang' => "en"}
  %head
    <meta http-equiv="Content-Type" content="text/html;
charset=UTF-8" />
    %title= @title || "Awesome Site"
  %body
    #wrapper
      #header
        %h1 Awesome Site
      #content= yield
      #footer
        %small Copyright Hampton Lintorn Catlin
```

Voilà. No more ugly DOCTYPE line. If you want a specific output type, you can always reference the Haml documentation for a complete list of variations.[4]

One more thing: comments. Just as with regular programming, good commenting is almost always a good idea. If we want to do a nonprinting comment (for example, something that we're only saying internally), then we can just do the following:

```
-# This comment won't print
```

Basically, the - means it's a nonprinting Ruby line, and the # is the standard Ruby form for comments. So it's just a little hack to do nonprinting comments.

What if you want real HTML comments? OK!

```
/ This is an HTML comment
```

This compiles to:

```
<!-- This is an HTML comment -->
```

---

4.   http://haml.info/docs/yardoc/file.REFERENCE.html

Index

Secure and Better JavaScript

Secure your Node applications and make writing JavaScript easier and more productive.

Secure Your Node.js Web Application

Cyber-criminals have your web applications in their crosshairs. They search for and exploit common security mistakes in your web application to steal user data. Learn how you can secure your Node.js applications, database and web server to avoid these security holes. Discover the primary attack vectors against web applications, and implement security best practices and effective countermeasures. Coding securely will make you a stronger web developer and analyst, and you'll protect your users.

Karl Düüna
(230 pages) ISBN: 9781680500851. $36
https://pragprog.com/book/kdnodesec

CoffeeScript

Over the last five years, CoffeeScript has taken the web development world by storm. With the humble motto "It's just JavaScript," CoffeeScript provides all the power of the JavaScript language in a friendly and elegant package. This extensively revised and updated new edition includes an all-new project to demonstrate CoffeeScript in action, both in the browser and on a Node.js server. There's no faster way to learn to write a modern web application.

Trevor Burnham
(124 pages) ISBN: 9781941222263. $29
https://pragprog.com/book/tbcoffee2

The Modern Web

Get up to speed on the latest JavaScript techniques.

Deliver Audacious Web Apps with Ember 2

It's time for web development to be fun again, time to write engaging and attractive apps – fast – in this brisk tutorial. Build a complete user interface in a few lines of code, create reusable web components, access RESTful services and cache the results for performance, and use JavaScript modules to bring abstraction to your code. Find out how you can get your crucial app infrastructure up and running quickly, so you can spend your time on the stuff great apps are made of: features.

Matthew White
(154 pages) ISBN: 9781680500783. $24
https://pragprog.com/book/mwjsember

Reactive Programming with RxJS

Reactive programming is revolutionary. It makes asynchronous programming clean, intuitive, and robust. Use the RxJS library to write complex programs in a simple way, unifying asynchronous mechanisms such as callbacks and promises into a powerful data type: the Observable. Learn to think about your programs as streams of data that you can transform by expressing *what* should happen, instead of having to painstakingly program *how* it should happen. Manage real-world concurrency and write complex flows of events in your applications with ease.

Sergi Mansilla
(142 pages) ISBN: 9781680501292. $18
https://pragprog.com/book/smreactjs

The Modern Web

Get up to speed on the latest HTML, CSS, and JavaScript techniques.

HTML5 and CSS3 (2nd edition)

HTML5 and CSS3 are more than just buzzwords—they're the foundation for today's web applications. This book gets you up to speed on the HTML5 elements and CSS3 features you can use right now in your current projects, with backwards compatible solutions that ensure that you don't leave users of older browsers behind. This new edition covers even more new features, including CSS animations, IndexedDB, and client-side validations.

Brian P. Hogan
(314 pages) ISBN: 9781937785598. $38
https://pragprog.com/book/bhh52e

Async JavaScript

With the advent of HTML5, front-end MVC, and Node.js, JavaScript is ubiquitous—and still messy. This book will give you a solid foundation for managing async tasks without losing your sanity in a tangle of callbacks. It's a fast-paced guide to the most essential techniques for dealing with async behavior, including PubSub, evented models, and Promises. With these tricks up your sleeve, you'll be better prepared to manage the complexity of large web apps and deliver responsive code.

Trevor Burnham
(104 pages) ISBN: 9781937785277. $17
https://pragprog.com/book/tbajs

Long Live the Command Line!

Use tmux and Vim for incredible mouse-free productivity.

tmux

Your mouse is slowing you down. The time you spend context switching between your editor and your consoles eats away at your productivity. Take control of your environment with tmux, a terminal multiplexer that you can tailor to your workflow. Learn how to customize, script, and leverage tmux's unique abilities and keep your fingers on your keyboard's home row.

Brian P. Hogan
(88 pages) ISBN: 9781934356968. $16.25
https://pragprog.com/book/bhtmux

Practical Vim, Second Edition

Vim is a fast and efficient text editor that will make you a faster and more efficient developer. It's available on almost every OS, and if you master the techniques in this book, you'll never need another text editor. In more than 120 Vim tips, you'll quickly learn the editor's core functionality and tackle your trickiest editing and writing tasks. This beloved bestseller has been revised and updated to Vim 7.4 and includes three brand-new tips and five fully revised tips.

Drew Neil
(354 pages) ISBN: 9781680501278. $29
https://pragprog.com/book/dnvim2

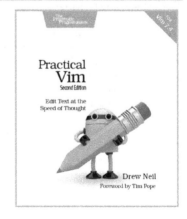

Put the "Fun" in Functional

Elixir 1.2 puts the "fun" back into functional programming, on top of the robust, battle-tested, industrial-strength environment of Erlang. Add in the unparalleled beauty and ease of the Phoenix web framework, and enjoy the web again!

Programming Elixir 1.2

You want to explore functional programming, but are put off by the academic feel (tell me about monads just one more time). You know you need concurrent applications, but also know these are almost impossible to get right. Meet Elixir, a functional, concurrent language built on the rock-solid Erlang VM. Elixir's pragmatic syntax and built-in support for metaprogramming will make you productive and keep you interested for the long haul. This book is *the* introduction to Elixir for experienced programmers.

Dave Thomas
(354 pages) ISBN: 9781680501667. $38
https://pragprog.com/book/elixir12

Programming Phoenix

Don't accept the compromise between fast and beautiful: you can have it all. Phoenix creator Chris McCord, Elixir creator José Valim, and award-winning author Bruce Tate walk you through building an application that's fast and reliable. At every step, you'll learn from the Phoenix creators not just what to do, but why. Packed with insider insights, this definitive guide will be your constant companion in your journey from Phoenix novice to expert, as you build the next generation of web applications.

Chris McCord, Bruce Tate, and José Valim
(298 pages) ISBN: 9781680501452. $34
https://pragprog.com/book/phoenix

The Pragmatic Bookshelf

The Pragmatic Bookshelf features books written by developers for developers. The titles continue the well-known Pragmatic Programmer style and continue to garner awards and rave reviews. As development gets more and more difficult, the Pragmatic Programmers will be there with more titles and products to help you stay on top of your game.

Visit Us Online

This Book's Home Page
https://pragprog.com/book/pg_sass3
Source code from this book, errata, and other resources. Come give us feedback, too!

Register for Updates
https://pragprog.com/updates
Be notified when updates and new books become available.

Join the Community
https://pragprog.com/community
Read our weblogs, join our online discussions, participate in our mailing list, interact with our wiki, and benefit from the experience of other Pragmatic Programmers.

New and Noteworthy
https://pragprog.com/news
Check out the latest pragmatic developments, new titles and other offerings.

Save on the eBook

Save on the eBook versions of this title. Owning the paper version of this book entitles you to purchase the electronic versions at a terrific discount.

PDFs are great for carrying around on your laptop—they are hyperlinked, have color, and are fully searchable. Most titles are also available for the iPhone and iPod touch, Amazon Kindle, and other popular e-book readers.

Buy now at *https://pragprog.com/coupon*

Contact Us

Online Orders:	*https://pragprog.com/catalog*
Customer Service:	*support@pragprog.com*
International Rights:	*translations@pragprog.com*
Academic Use:	*academic@pragprog.com*
Write for Us:	*http://write-for-us.pragprog.com*
Or Call:	+1 800-699-7764

Milton Keynes UK
Ingram Content Group UK Ltd.
UKHW021822180923
428919UK00011B/609